The Mys...
FINAL F...GHT
of
MH-370

The most fascinating, anomalous mystery disappearance in a century—since the sinking of the Titanic!

An enlightened observer's diary of the chronological, historical facts surrounding the tragic loss of missing Malaysia Airlines flight no. MH-370, a Boeing 777 - 200 series

ROBERT DOMINGUEZ

ISBN 978-1-64258-783-8 (paperback)
ISBN 978-1-64258-784-5 (digital)

Christian Faith Publishing, Inc.
832 Park Avenue
Meadville, PA 16335
www.christianfaithpublishing.com

Originally published: © December 12, 2014

Printed in the United States of America

DISCLAIMER

The author *does not* claim the entirety of this chronological, historical diary to be 100 percent scientifically accurate, in that

A) certain names may not be correctly spelled;
B) some of the job titles and/or job descriptions may not be totally and exactly correct;
C) some of the dimensions, figures, and numbers may be approximated and not scientifically or perfectly exact.

The author and artist, Robert Dominguez, offers his apologies to those concerned.

Also, the author and artist *does offer* his condolences and compassionate sympathies to the 239 victims of Malaysia Airlines flight no. MH-370 and to all the surviving family members, friends, and associates of these victims, and including the MA flight no. MH-17 disaster mentioned in my addendum.

DEDICATION

This nonfiction, factually fascinating, historical chronology of the tragic loss of Malaysia Airlines flight no. MH-370, a Boeing 777-200, is dedicated to the 239 victims listed on the passenger and flight crew manifests as well as all the members of their surviving families, friends, and associates.

I also dedicate this manuscript to my precious daughter, Jennifer Ann, my two grandsons, Brendan Robert and Raymond Joseph, and my late wife, Debra Lee, and my two late sons, Joseph Smith and Jonathan Robert.

SPECIAL THANKS

To all the scientists, engineers, mathematicians, captains, pilots, explorers, technologists, and aviation analysts (interviewed by journalists in association with Cable News Network [CNN], Time-Warner Co., and Turner Entertainment Group Co.), all professionals associated with; Inmarsat Satellite Company, Boeing Company, Woods-Hole Oceanographic Institute, The US Navy, The Australian Navy, The Chinese Navy, The Bangladesh Navy, and all others directly (search teams and explorers) or indirectly involved in the search for missing Malaysia Airlines flight No. MH-370.

CONTENTS

ILLUSTRATIONS
AND CHARTS

The World

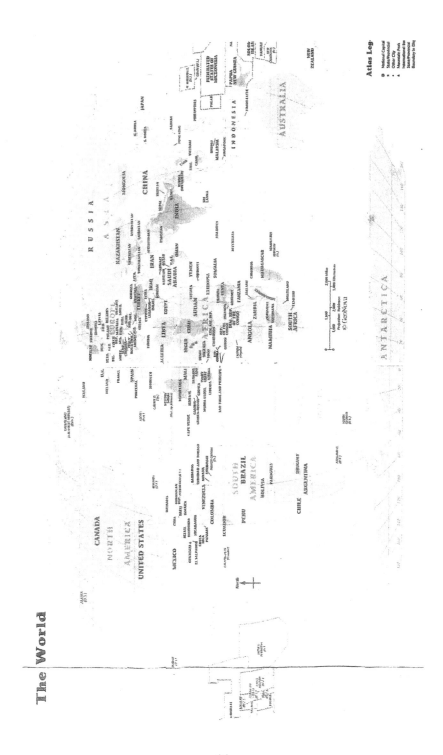

The World

12

Russia, Ukraine and Asia

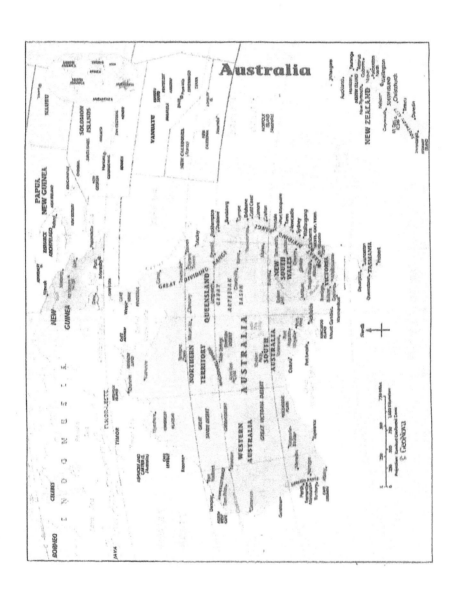

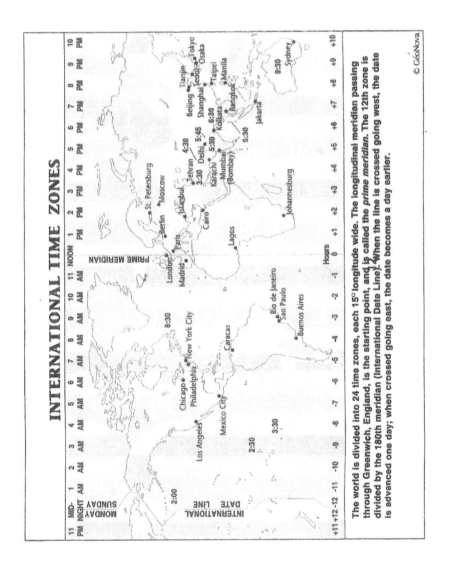

INTERNATIONAL TIME ZONES

The world is divided into 24 time zones, each 15° longitude wide. The longitudinal meridian passing through Greenwich, England, is the starting point, and is called the *prime meridian*. The 12th zone is divided by the 180th meridian (International Date Line). When the line is crossed going west, the date is advanced one day; when crossed going east, the date becomes a day earlier.

© GeoNova

PROLOGUE

The fate of the final flight of MA flight no. MH-370 seems
a reminder of the adage "God giveth and God taketh away."
God giving is a blessing, and oddly, God taketh away may
possibly be another blessing disguised in a reverse way.

In the vastness of our known and unknown universe,
it seems our Earth is known and unknown.

In the vastness of our universe, it seems evident that
all we Earthlings on our planet Earth are only but
ants within the big picture of our universe.

But very intelligent and curious Earthly human ants!

Robert Dominguez, author and artist
And now, please ponder *The Mysterious Final Flight of MH-370*.

P A R T 1

As Boeing-777 200 Series Captain Shah and his First Officer, Fariq Hamid, labored in the cockpit, busy making sense of B-777's safety checklists and the usual communications with the control tower at Kuala Lumpur International Airport in Malaysia, the public address loudspeakers announced, "Please begin boarding Malaysia Airlines flight no. MH-370, destination Beijing, China." Looking at her wristwatch, reading 12:00 AM (midnight), she added, "Thank you for your cooperation and enjoy your flight aboard Malaysia Airlines. Thank you."

This is a normally scheduled "red eye" flight. 12:32 AM, taxiing. 12:42 AM, departure from Kuala Lumpur with a 6:30 AM Beijing arrival. A route flown many times by the highly regarded Captain Shah himself, sporting approximately eighteen thousand hours of experience in the aircraft left-hand Captain's Seat. And a relief to Malaysia Airlines.

However, in the cockpit's right-hand Seat sat a relatively new co-pilot to assist in the flight of the enormous, wide-bodied Boeing-777. He got this position by flying many hours of Boeing-737 transport.

And although on his third B-777 flight, with the highly-reputable Captain Shah, he would soon face discipline for photographing himself with two girls in the B-737 cockpit in flight!

However, discipline would be meted out at a later date. Presently, he is assisting Captain Shah with the pre-flight duties of his job description, as 227 paying passengers walked the skyway to board the Boeing-777's gigantic fuselage and hunt for their seats printed on their boarding passes.

Two hundred twenty six paying passengers were co-joined with Mr. Phillip Wood, an American flying to Beijing, seeking a construction job near the China-Mongolia region of the Earth. Mr. Wood, probably preoccupied with normal thoughts of successfully benefiting his own family, by working his potential job assignment, located his seat, sat, and reclined.

All other passengers may have been embarking on similar endeavors, while others were to vacation and others to reunite with their beloved family members, friends, and homes.

The ten flight attendants, having received notice of a completely boarded passenger manifest, closed, sealed, and locked for flight purposes the fuselage doors.

Meanwhile, the ground crew scrambled, as normal, to complete fueling as well as baggage and cargo loading responsibilities in order to close all their respective openings to seal the fuselage for departure, take-off, and flight.

PART 2

After taxiing to the main runway, Captain Shah and his co-pilot received tower clearance for take-off. Then, as usual, Captain Shah revs up by throttling his twin Rolls Royce engines to 100 percent and then releasing the brakes on all three landing gears.

With flaps properly positioned, the well-designed and well-built Boeing-777 thrust its passengers' back, as the decade-old airframe rocketed forward, thanks to the power of his engines' screaming. With gauges and indicators in the green, Captain Shah, done steering, pulls back on the control stick, and his B-777's tail horizontal stabilizer elevators pitched, thereby enabling pointing the nose up, as the mighty thrust provided lift, thanks to the modern airfoil design of his wings.

All normal. Everything normal. All instrumentation, indicators, communications, *all* normal, as the flight crew arrives at the critically precious altitude of four hundred feet.

After clearing Kuala Lumpur International Airport and constantly gaining the obligatory lift, the flight crew in the Boeing-777 cockpit begin maneuvering to obtain a northerly heading for a destination landing in Beijing, China. All normal, *but was it?*

Everything normal, but *no* arrival in China!

PART 3

No normal 6:30 AM (Beijing time zone) arrival in China! *Why?* What happened? Two Iranian citizens somehow boarded MA flight no. MH-370 with two stolen passports. A factor?

In Beijing, China, family members and friends awaiting flight no. MH-370 at Beijing International Airport are bewildered and in a state of utter shock! And in Kuala Lumpur, Malaysia, family members and friends are equally bewildered, and also in a state of similar utter shock! In Kuala Lumpur, Malaysia Airlines must be in a state of confusion as well! Confusion in Malaysia because flight no. MH-370 is owned by them (by nationalization).

In the United States, the family and girlfriend of Phillip Wood are in wonderment! It resembles a cruelly and unusually executed modern-Day "Now you see it, now you don't." It's only a six-hour flight from Kuala Lumpur to Beijing. *Where is it?*

Families and friends in China, Malaysia, and the USA wondering why the Boeing-777 *never landed* in Beijing, ask, how? Why? Where? The world now wants to know the whereabouts of MA flight no. MH-370. And so, the world begins scouring all news reports to learn if flight no. MH-370 diverted and is now elsewhere. Some people tune in to Cable News Network (CNN).

PART 4

At Cable News Network (CNN), a genuine effort is performed to verify the accuracy of news *prior* to reporting and broadcasting details. Most reputable news bureaus do. Anchorman Mr. John Berman *is first* to announce the initial report, saying, "Just in. A Malaysia Airlines Boeing-777 departing Kuala Lumpur, Malaysia, has failed to arrive at its destination of Beijing, China."

Because our Earth rotates west to east, our Earth is divided into twenty-four time zones to match our twenty-four-hour day and night globally. Since each new day begins at the "imaginary" international date line, located on the Western Pacific Ocean, we in the Eastern United States are exactly twelve hours behind the Malaysia time zone.

Naturally: It is twelve hours earlier in Malaysia, while at the same moment, it is twelve hours later in the Eastern Standard Time (EST) zone of the USA, and during the summer season, forty-eight of our fifty states in the US utilize daylight savings time (DST). Therefore, when it is 6:00 PM in Malaysia, it is 6:00 AM in the Eastern Standard Time (EST) Zone of The United States.

Example: Malaysia, Saturday, March 8, 2014, 3:00 AM
= USA (EST), Friday, March 7, 2014, 3:00 PM.

Most time of day(s) cited within this chronological, historical diary may be referenced using Eastern Standard Time (EST) and/or Daylight Savings Time (EDT) during our US summer season daylight savings time period.

PART 5

On day no. 1 of the disappearance of Malaysia Airlines flight no. MH-370, the Boeing-777 departed Kuala Lumpur International Airport in Malaysia at 12:32 to 12:42 AM on Saturday, March 8, 2014, MST (Malaysia Standard Time), and flight no. MH-370 was due to land six hours later at its destination in Beijing, China, at 6:30 AM. However, unfortunately, flight no. MH-370 *never arrived* in Beijing. Some passengers would have deplaned, while new passengers would have then boarded, as flight 370 was a scheduled continuing flight with other Asian final destinations. All the remainder of the day (of the flight) and into the night, family members and friends and associates of the missing aircraft remained in a state of shock. *Where* is flight 370 and what happened to its passengers?

So on day no. 2, Saturday, March 8, 2014, EST (Eastern Standard Time), Malaysia Airlines announces, "Flight 370 is now officially missing. We do not know of its location, nor its circumstances." And so, the anomalous, mysterious disappearance officially begins, with such an official announcement, made by its owner, Malaysia Airlines Company.

The next day, it becomes day no. 3 (EST) in the eastern hemisphere of the Earth (and simultaneously, day no. 2 in the western hemisphere of our Earth), when Cable News Network (CNN) announces, "BREAKING NEWS. A Malaysia Airlines Boeing-777, with (239) crew and passengers, departing Kuala Lumpur, Malaysia, has *failed* to arrive at its scheduled destination of Beijing, China."

Two days later, on Tuesday, March 11, 2014, and day no. 5 since flight 370 disappeared, CNN again now announces, by Broadcast Video Billboard, "Breaking News: The Mystery of flight 370—STILL

MISSING." It is 1:00 PM (EST). Mr. Wolf Blitzer says CNN has dispatched correspondents to all the cities and countries involved. He then interviews Mr. Tom Forman one-half hour later, who, through the use of virtual imaging techniques, demonstrates to their worldwide audience the logistics of the intended flight path of the missing Boeing-777.

After interviewing Mr. Forman, Mr. Blitzer speaks about upcoming, future expert input from invited aviation analysts, engineers, scientists, mathematicians, pilots, and others having aviation experience and expertise. And sure enough, the next day, Wednesday, March 12, 2014, day no. 6 of the missing Boeing-777, Mr. Blitzer interviews two invited experts to present scientific facts, buttressed with computer-generated imaging, pertaining to the course of missing MA flight no. MH-370. Additionally, Mr. Tom Forman, using virtual imaging, showed the relationship between the Indian Ocean and missing flight 370.

Furthermore, Mr. Blitzer interviewed two other guests. One was Mr. Richard Quest (CNN aviation analyst), as well as his other guest, an experienced Boeing-777 captain. They both offered their viewpoints concerning the disappearance of the Boeing-777. Later that day, Mr. Jake Tapper, anchorman of CNN's Newscast, invited Mr. Michael Goldfarb, former federal aviation administration (FAA) chief of staff, to discuss the propagation of cracks, found on some Boeing-777s. Mr. Goldfarb replied that the issuing of airworthiness directives are then sent to all operators of the Boeing-777 worldwide.

An airworthiness directive (AD), dealing with the structural integrity of an aircraft is science and engineering reporting, issued in an effort to prevent the compromising of aircraft structural integrity to aviation mechanics and maintenance crews to address either potential airframe corrosion and/or other engineering factors involved, including mechanical repair, ultimately for/with aircraft in flight safety for passengers, flight crew, and cargo. During the last nineteen years, over 1,200 Boeing-777s have been sold internationally, moving millions of passengers safely, while at least one hundred airworthiness directives (ADs) were issued.

PART 6

Now, it is being reported, three days after the fact that a Chinese satellite image may contribute to the solving of missing Malaysia Airlines flight no. MH-370. The image was released by The Chinese Institute of Science, Technology, and Industry. So CNN's Mr. Jake Tapper is now interviewing Mr. Peter Goelz, former National Transportation and Safety Board (NTSB) managing director, who is stating that the Chinese satellite image "is indicative of an *aeronautical problem*." Next, he is giving three approximate dimensions of the three images of the potential wreckage floating between Malaysia and Vietnam, seen by the Chinese satellite.

Correlating with Peter Goelz, is CNN International correspondent Mr. Jim Sciutto, reporting on the dimensions of a Boeing-777, obtained from a Boeing aircraft blueprint. The dimensions of a Boeing-777 are as follows: (drawing below *not* to scale);

Fuselage Length = 200 feet / Wingtip to wingtip = 200 feet

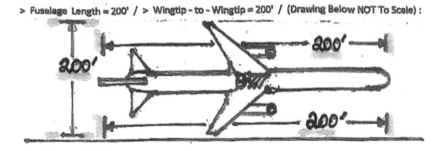

Finally, on day 6 of the missing MA flight no. MH-370, Wednesday, March 12, 2014 (EST), Mr. Richard Quest and Mr. Patrick Smith discuss the possibilities of the three pieces of floating objects spotted by the Chinese satellite three days earlier, matching the dimensions of the Boeing-777 blueprint. The Chinese satellite images can only be approximated. Boeing-777 pilot Mr. Keith Wolzinger also contributed to today's analysis discussed. The body of ocean where the three pieces of floating potential wreckage were spotted by the Chinese satellite may have been in, or the vicinity of, the South China Sea, bordering the coasts of both Malaysia and Vietnam.

The Vietnam control tower area was to communicate with flight 370 after their signing off with the Malaysian control tower at the point of departure, Kuala Lumpur Airport. Is it possible that the three pieces of floating potential wreckage are authentic? Then, location of the missing Boeing-777 main wreckage could be isolated! All based on drift and ocean current variables. And aircraft with passengers found? This would be a tremendous leap forward in the search for missing flight 370!

The three pieces of floating objects spotted by the Chinese satellite images will not be verified until a fly-over by rescue aircraft locate the position of the three objects. Then rescue ships will be dispatched to seize the three objects to learn if they are in fact genuine Boeing-777-styled aircraft wreckage.

PART 7

Two days later, Friday, March 14, 2014 (EST), it is now day 8 since the disappearance of flight 370, which had five thousand pounds of *lithium batteries* as cargo within its cargo bay! Mr. Don Lemon, CNN anchorman, is concluding a theoretical version of events, concerning the danger(s) of *lithium batteries* on board (which may have ignited, causing fire), with a panel of three experts. Interestingly, such a scenario has been recently plaguing Boeing Aircraft Co.'s newest aircraft: the Boeing-787 Dreamliner (which uses *lithium batteries*). *Lithium batteries* may accidentally overheat and cause a fire if not properly stored, whether in use on board or simply being transported within the aircraft cargo bay.

Also, Mr. Lemon is now interviewing Mr. Brian Todd, correspondent, who is reporting on the occurrence of a geological seismic event that took place under the ocean in the general area where flight 370 may have first disappeared. This report leads to speculation on the manner, in which changed ocean currents, and/or tides, may have an effect on the drifting wreckage of a downed aircraft in the open ocean, possibly causing greater difficulty for search aircraft to find the spotted three pieces of floating debris found by the Chinese satellite.

PART 8

Now, on day no. 12, Tuesday, March 18, 2014 (EST), Ms. Brooke Baldwin, CNN anchorwoman, has introduced Mr. Chad Myers, meteorologist. Mr. Myers is now reporting on visual sightings by a few "witnesses," who claimed they viewed flight 370 in flight near the Maldives island chain or to the east over water, pointing out there is no adequately-lengthened runway to permit the landing of a huge aircraft. These alleged "witnesses" claim their viewing occurred on March 8, 2014, MST (Malaysia Standard Time Zone) or March 7, 2014 (US EST), the day no. 1 of the flight of missing MA flight no. MH-370.

For this to take place, the flight crew, after leaving Malaysia, and bidding the Kuala Lumpur Airport control tower good night, would have had to redirect flight no. MH-370 West, by making an in-flight left-hand turn (port) over the South China Sea, before contacting the next control tower located at Ho Chi Minh City in South Vietnam. Then, flying west over South Thailand, but north of Indonesia flight no. MH-370's crew, would then have to maneuver an additional left-hand turn (port) to obtain a southerly heading. Then, above the Indian Ocean, such a sighting *may or may not* have occurred, *all* depending on flight no. MH-370's altitude.

Later, on day no. 12 of the missing Boeing-777, March 18, 2014 (EST), Ms. Erin Burnett, CNN anchorwoman, interviewed Mr. Miles O'Brien, a pilot. Mr. O'Brien was previously CNN chief science correspondent, who usually reported from Cape Kennedy at Cape Canaveral, Florida, on US space shuttle missions, before moving to Public Broadcasting System (PBS) as chief science corre-spondent. Today, Ms. Burnett has reintroduced and welcomed Miles

O'Brien to participate in the analysis of the search for missing flight no. MH-370.

Three days later, day no. 15, Friday, March 21, 2014 (EST), Mr. Miles O'Brien reappeared on both Ms. Ashleigh Banfield's and Ms. Brooke Baldwin's CNN newscasts. On both newscasts, Miles O'Brien, being a licensed pilot, offered brilliant analysis on known facts of evidence involving the disappearance of Malaysia Airlines flight no. MH-370, speaking in a scientific manner. Unfortunately, not even the scientific analysis of Miles O'Brien has revealed the location of flight 370. Questions asked by a curious international flying public have *no* definite answers as yet, and flight 370 remains missing, now for fifteen days. The international public continues to ask, *why, how,* and *where?*

PART 9

F ive days have elapsed, bringing day no. 17 to the forefront. Now, during seventeen days of absence, not even the true flight path of the missing Boeing-777 is factually and accurately known. As of today, Sunday, March 23, 2014 (EST), radar reports observing flight 370 have been freely released. Radar information from Indonesia have not, either for political or for security/military reasons. The radar path of flight 370 has *gaps* and the mysterious disappearance of MA flight no. MH-370 *has not* been solved. The world continues to wonder!

Mr. Don Lemon, also curious, invites Mr. Chad Myers to respond with more knowledge on the subject of where is flight 370? Chad Myers now offers an explanation of "aircraft shadowing," whereby at altitude (or cruising elevation), an aircraft may conceal itself within the radar "blip," emitted by an unwitting Lead Aircraft, already en route on its flight path to whichever destination The Lead Aircraft is headed. The second aircraft (the "shadowing aircraft") merely flies just behind and just above the Lead Aircraft, but with its transponder turned to the *off* position. Radar, as it is engineered to function, only reads one (1) "blip" = the "blip" of the Lead Aircraft that *does* have their transponder turned on.

Mysteriously, for some unknown reason, MA flight no. MH-370, after radioing good night to the Kuala Lumpur International Airport control tower and prior to entering Vietnamese airspace suddenly and abruptly turned off their transponder, and other redundant safety devices, such as ACAR (Aircraft Communication, Alerting, and Reporting) / ACART (Aircraft Communication, Alerting, and

Reporting Transmission), and safety positioning device(s) were also turned off, thereby becoming an unknown *"ghost ship"!*

The purpose of aircraft transponders is to readily and easily identify themselves to all-radar stations. For example, the transponder identifies if it is a military or civilian aircraft. It also transmits valuable information such as type or size of the aircraft, its tail identification number (N number in USA), plus other data beneficial to its safety, down to ground-based control towers and radar systems (or up to orbiting satellites). In case of in-flight emergency, the aircraft can be located and help provided.

The ACAR/ACART Safety Positioning Device(s), wired electrically to each engine, reports and transmits, important information, such as engine efficiency, fuel quantity, and engine fuel starvation.

On departure from Kuala Lumpur, Malaysia, flight 370's transponder was on. Normal flight operation.

Why was flight 370's transponder turned off? Was it intentional or was it caused by mechanical malfunction? These questions mystify the flying public and world!

The profundity of the mystery of missing MA flight no. MH-370 deepens!

PART 10

It's Monday, March 24, 2014 (EST), and it is day no. 18 that flight 370 has been missing! Now reporting is Miles O'Brien, pilot and aviation analyst, describing, according to available radar information, flight 370's rapid descent down to an altitude of twelve thousand feet from as high as forty-five thousand feet. Does this demonstrate a catastrophic event whereby passenger cabin pressurization may have been compromised by an emergency situation? Or did *others* tamper, not only with the aircraft's transponder, but also with the aircraft's rapid descent from a normal cruise altitude, by entering the flight cabin (cockpit)? Passengers, as well as anyone, have much difficulty absorbing oxygen into all minute areas of the lungs where carbon dioxide is exchanged for incoming, fresh, and life-giving oxygen due to low atmospheric pressure(s) encountered at elevations above eleven thousand or twelve thousand feet of altitude and leading to hypoxia.

Meanwhile, search aircraft as well as search ships for longer than the last two weeks have been combing both the South China Sea and the Andaman Sea (west of Thailand), in hopes of possibly locating downed and floating pieces of identifiable Boeing-777 aircraft wreckage. *Alas, no wreckage found yet!*

PART 11

Later, on day no. 18, Monday, March 24, 2014 (EST), anchor-woman Ms. Brooke Baldwin invites two journalists to inquire and explain "Doppler shift." Meteorologist Chad Myers speaks first on the subject. Tom Forman secondly. "Doppler shift" is a scientific method, by which, the British-owned Inmarsat satellite company, determined and confirmed that the flight path of missing flight no. MH-370 did have a final southerly heading of direction because Inmarsat's satellite is geo-synchronous or stationary (in the same spot in space over the same spot of the Earth), while in earthly orbit in space. This fact, thereby, gives an indication of the final communicating "pings" between Inmarsat's satellite and/with the vanished Boeing-777, demonstrating missing flight no. MH-370 distanced itself—in fact, in a southerly heading of direction, from the geo-synchronous Inmarsat satellite.

Next, Tom Forman (in combination with virtual imaging), explains *how* the Inmarsat geo-synchronous satellite was able to determine and confirm, that the missing Malaysia Airlines flight no. MH-370 flew south. Mr. Forman, with more virtual imaging, then gave a mathematical formula used by scientists at Inmarsat satellite company to mathematically prove the vanished Boeing-777 flew south, into the Southern Indian Ocean.

With further virtual imaging, Tom showed simultaneously, the Inmarsat satellite in its geo-synchronous Earth orbit, and also the positioning of flight 370 aircraft locations flying south, to the Southern Indian Ocean, by using geometric 360° circles, all at various latitudes, to explain mathematically, why this, the Southern

Indian Ocean, is the final destination and resting place of MA flight no. MH-370.

Finally, on day no. 18, Mr. Ed Lavandera, CNN correspondent, invited by Don Lemon, reports that magnesium, placed into an ocean/brine environment, can/may dissolve, similarly "to an Alka-Seltzer tablet in water." This has importance, in that, aircraft use magnesium as a vital metallic alloying component to strengthen and lengthen the service life of an aircraft.

Remember, the missing flight no. MH-370 may have ditched into seawater. It never landed in China nor any other international airport. And the search aircraft and search ships, are still on the hunt for the missing Boeing-777, and its 239 passengers and crew. *All seem to have vanished!*

PART 12

It is now day no. 19 of the disappearance of Malaysia Airlines flight no. MH-370, and Tuesday, March 25, 2014 (EST). CNN's anchorwoman Ms. Ashleigh Banfield has invited and convened a three person panel of aviation analysts including Richard Quest. Mr. Quest mentioned the mathematical formula, involved in the "Doppler shift," that was instrumental for Inmarsat Satellite Company scientists to deduce, that the missing flight no. MH-370 did embark on a southerly heading toward and onto/into, the South Indian Ocean.

One of the two experts explained mathematically, through the use of charts and diagrams, the differing wavelengths of the outbound satellite "ping," and the return "ping" from the aircraft flight no. MH-370. The charts visually demonstrate the compression of the wavelengths, or lack thereof. In total, six and one half "pings" were detected. Was the final half "ping," when flight 370 made contact with the Earth and/or ocean?

Based on the findings of the Inmarsat satellites' six and a half pingings, transmitted to and received from flight no. MH-370, both aerial and surface ship searches must continue for three primary reasons:

A) The vanished 239 passengers and crew, all have concerned surviving family members, friends, and associates who wonder about their well-being and their whereabouts.

B) The flying public deserves to know the cause of the disappearance, just as the remainder of the international populace desires the answers, of how and why flight 370 is missing, including Malaysia, owner of Nationalized Malaysia Airlines.

C) Boeing aircraft manufacturing company must be curious about the safety and reliability of the other 1,200 Boeing-777s already designed, constructed, sold, and flown daily transcontinentally, transoceanically, and internationally. (Each can sell for $ 250,000,000.)

Later on day no. 19, Ms. Brooke Baldwin invites and interviews Mr. David Soucie, author of *Why Planes Crash*, on the topic of the two on-board "black boxes." (So-called "black boxes" are actually painted orange in color). David Soucie is explaining that the *ping* beacons of "black boxes," emit "pings" for location purposes, once per second, at a certain and particular frequency, unlike any natural source. Also, this frequency differs from that of all other man-made electronic devices. In this manner, pinger locator devices can "zero in" for aircraft recovery purposes.

Meanwhile, Mr. Martin Savidge, a CNN correspondent, has, for several days, been working together with Mr. Mitchell Quesada, a Boeing-777 flight simulator instructor, and is reporting from inside such a Boeing-777 cockpit, within the flight simulator. This is very close co-operation, which replicates the actual environment that B-777 captains and their first officers (co-pilots) work in, to fly, control, and maneuver such aircraft. Also, speculation surrounding those events, leading to the disappearance of flight no. MH-370 can be more closely examined, from behind the controls of that massive and giant Boeing-777 aircraft flight simulator.

Incidentally, as to the two "black boxes" on board MH-370, their separate batteries are able to operate totally independent of any aircraft connectivity, which raises the question of battery life or duration of electrical charge, underwater. "Black box" battery life or battery charge duration is estimated to be a minimum of thirty days to a maximum of forty days, dependent on various factors. ("Black box" batteries power the ping beacon.) Such critical factors concerning "black box" battery-charge longevity (life) may include the following:

a) Quality of battery storage environment,
b) Voltage charge capacity and quantity,
c) Age of existing battery and condition,
d) Any potential damage from impact (crash).

PART 13

Today is day no. 20, Wednesday, March 26, 2014 (EST), and flight no. MH-370 has been missing almost three weeks now. Three days ago on Sunday, a French satellite has sighted 122 items and/or pieces of potential wreckage. But is it Boeing-777 aircraft wreckage? The world hopes: yes! Using virtual imaging techniques, Mr. Tom Forman is providing a truly great scientific report. By using his virtual imaging, Tom is clearly explaining the search objectives by superimposing a virtual grid of the Earth in relation to the floating objects.

However, the science of ocean drift would need to be reverse-engineered to determine the approximate location of impact twenty days ago. Now, Mr. Nicholas Mallos, an oceanographer, and an expert on ocean-surface debris and flotsam for the Ocean Conservancy Group, is explaining how ocean debris scatters by ocean currents, ocean gyres, and other scientifically technical reasonings. He is explaining to Ms. Ashleigh Banfield, CNN anchorwoman, that an ocean gyre is a whirlpool in which water moving rapidly in a circular motion may produce a depression in its center into which floating objects may be drawn in.

Later, Wolf Blitzer interviews Mr. Mark Weiss, Boeing-777 pilot, Mr. Tom Fuentes, former US FBI investigator, and a third aviation analyst, concerning the ramifications involved in the disappearance of flight 370. Mr. Fuentes connects the aircrafts' behavior to a potential crime, if a terrorist had indeed entered the flight cabin (cockpit) to commandeer the Boeing-777 or if the flight crew itself intentionally turned off the aircrafts' transponder, in order to divert without emergency. Mr. Weiss, B-777 pilot, spoke of the reliability, Boeing manufacturing company has engineered into the various safety systems on board such modern aircraft. The third aviation analyst downplayed the speculation, or rumors, some have circulated, in which unidentified flying objects (UFOs) intervened by snatching the vanished flight 370.

Now, Mr. Ryan Abernathy, of Columbia University, is stating the 122 objects sighted by the French satellite in the area of the Indian Ocean, do correspond and correlate with the behavior of downed aircraft floating wreckage.

And the *saga of the search* for missing flight 370 by dedicated search aircraft and search ships courageously continues, moving from the South China and Andaman Seas, and now searching for aircraft wreckage concentrated in the Indian Ocean, based on Inmarsat's satellites and the French satellite sighting.

Assuredly, this daily search plys on almost religiously, in that there are 239 passengers and crew members missing. Not only do their surviving families and friends want answers in the form of physical evidence, but so does the world's flying public of paying passengers, flight crews, and all other curious persons, also desiring physical evidence and facts.

Later, on the same day no. 20, Ms. Brooke Baldwin is now examining the "partial ping," that arrived eight minutes after the last normal ping communication, between the Inmarsat satellite and the missing Boeing-777. The eight-minute span of time could possibly help pinpoint the potential "crash site." Note: When the Inmarsat satellite company reported the six and one-half pings. The half ping and the abnormal "partial ping," are both the one and the same partial ping.

However, Boeing-777 pilot Mr. Les Abend is stating, in his opinion, that mechanical failure is the most probable cause for the disappearance of flight 370. Also, he addressed the "partial ping," not to be caused by ocean impact by flight 370, but rather, by the engineering involved, when an aircraft runs low or out of fuel, leading to its electrical bus circuitry being co-linked to its twin Rolls-Royce engines, that may/can be affected/effected, thereby causing "partial pinging."

Adding to the 122 objects sighted by the French satellite is Mr. Leo Romejin, a satellite imaging analyst, who is now discussing "sun reflectivity" (i.e., reflections caused by our sun). Also, Leo states that some commercial satellites have a double daily orbit of our Earth, in association, with a double daily orbit over the Indian Ocean. Would this fact assist tracing the direction of ocean drift, pertaining to possible flight 370, Boeing-777, aircraft floating wreckage?

Expert Mr. Ian MacDonald is now presenting the theory of "two intersecting processes of uncertainty." It is a scientific theory of positive identification between ocean flotsam and its relationship with ocean gyres. Gyres are naturally occurring whirlpools that exist in the oceans. Sadly, some ocean gyres fill with man-made garbage and rubbish.

Ms. Rosa Flores, a CNN correspondent, is now showing a visual demonstration of the ocean-surface launching of a high-tech unmanned AUV (autonomous underwater vehicle), that features a side scan radar capable of mapping the ocean floor.

Its side-scan radar can differentiate between smooth ocean floor and underwater mountains and valleys, as compared to the distinctive shape of a submerged aircraft or aircraft components. Note: The shape/form of an aircraft main landing gear differs greatly from the natural under-ocean layout or the natural design of our Earth.

Now, Ms. Baldwin is interviewing one family member, surviving one of the 239 missing passengers of the vanished flight 370. He desires actual facts and visual evidence of the missing Boeing-777. Still, he remains uncertain of pilot-error or of a human intervention in the flight cabin (cockpit), leading to tampering or even hi-jacking of the aircraft. He is untrusting of governmental secrecy existing in Malaysia. Yet on day no. 20, *USA Today* newspaper is reporting in an article: "That Captain Shah, piloting missing Malaysia Airlines flight no. MH-370, *'deliberately redirected'* the course of the vanished Boeing-777, due to the mental or psychological status of the captain."

It is being disclosed one item of the 122 pieces of debris sighted by the French satellite is the size of an aircraft wing.

However, Ms. Colleen Keller, senior analyst for Metron Inc., says while weather forecast is easily accomplished, underwater ocean current movement *cannot* be forecast. Luckily, improved weather conditions over the Indian Ocean search area, west of the continent of Australia, has allowed for all-day aerial searching, as well as search-ship exploration, on day no. 20 for missing MA flight no. MH-370.

And the search continues by twenty search aircraft and five search-ships, all sent by an existing coalition of twelve different nations. *But nothing yet found!*

Again, with no physical evidence found of MA flight no. MH-370, after three weeks of searching and technical analysis, the *profundity* of the Boeing-777 mystery disappearance is *deepening!*

PART 14

Weather conditions above the Indian Ocean often worsen. This occurred the following day, Thursday, March 27, 2014 (EST), and day no. 21 of flight 370's disappearance. Mr. Will Ripley, reporting from Perth, Australia, is stating today's search will be cut short, due to bad incoming weather over the search area "grid," superimposed onto the Indian Ocean. The aerial and ship searches will resume at 6:00 AM tomorrow morning, Friday, March 28, 2014 (EST). That is the equivalent of 6:00 AM in Perth, Australia. But more inclement weather is forecast to reform in the afternoon. So Thursday's search will be limited to half a day, as will Friday's half-day search.

Meanwhile, Ms. Ashleigh Banfield is reporting, Mr. David Soucie is now stating that the battery life, within both "black boxes," may have been compromised. Improper storage procedures by Malaysia Airlines may have negatively shortened the life span of the two "black boxes' batteries," and thereby resulting in reduced "black box ping" emission duration, from their two separate "ping beacons." This would challenge the ping locator device to scramble hurriedly before black box battery electrical power expires.

Now, 2:00 PM (EST), Ms. Brooke Baldwin says a Japanese satellite has spotted ten items/objects floating on the Indian Ocean, which may be potential aircraft wreckage. Additionally, ocean debris specialist Mr. Nicholas Mallos is also stating that a Thai satellite has now sighted 120 fragments of debris. Nicholas adds a fact of importance: as the ocean currents of the Indian Ocean move around, there exists a chance possibility, that some of the in-space satellites, might be viewing, a portion of, the same Flotsam.

43

Next, Mr. Chad Myers, CNN meteorologist, on the topic of wreckage sightings, says some geo-synchronous orbiting satellites, above this area of the Indian Ocean, obtain a forty-five degree-angled view to photograph. Whereas, conversely, the viewing advantages gained from pole to pole (polar) longitudinally orbiting satellites, may be able to obtain direct (straightly down), overhead views of the Flotsam, depending on the factoring in of the daily rotation of our Earth, in relation to which line of longitude, such A pole to pole orbiting satellite may possess, to better identify such Flotsam!

An Australian announcement, broadcast by Mr. Anderson Cooper, CNN anchorman, speaks of a new search field, located 680 miles to the northeast (NE) of yesterday's previous search area. This new search area happens to lie within a much friendlier area of the Indian Ocean, replete with Milder Tiding Effect, as well as, more favorable, milder weather.

This new search area is also nearly seven hundred miles northeast (NE) of what is popularly referred to as "The Roaring Forties," or the fortieth line of south latitude. Incidentally, ten degrees to the south of "The Roaring Forties" is what is popularly referred to as "The Screeching Fifties," or the fiftieth line of south latitude. And similarly, ten more degrees to the south of "The Screeching Fifties" is what is popularly referred to as "The Screaming Sixties," or The Sixtieth Line of South Latitude.

The reason for the above-mentioned three nicknames is the horribly stormy and windy weather frequently encountered between the south fortieth degree of latitude to the sixtieth degree of south latitude. Interestingly, ten more degrees to the south of "The Screaming Sixties," one is on the seventieth line of south latitude or the geo-physical perimeter of the continent of Antarctica! One would be standing on the icy surface of Antarctica itself!

Commander William Marks of the United States Navy remains very optimistic as to the condition of his sailors' on-duty searching ability, saying, "These missions and others is that which we all train for."

Lastly, now the estimated speed of the missing Boeing-777 has been downgraded from 450 knots to 400 knots. This is thanks to panels of experts continuing the computerized analysis of preexisting radar sighting points in the search for missing flight 370.

Speaking of downgraded airspeed, this is the plight of many of the search aircraft:

* Firstly, search aircraft must fly hundreds of miles from an Australian airbase to arrive at the search area(s) over the Southern Indian Ocean. (There are two search areas longitudinally-opposed: one north and one south.)

* Secondly, they must fly slowly, and sometimes turning off one of their engines to not risk overflying a potential wreckage fragment and if not sighting the/an object, perhaps omitting a piece of the puzzle, that might solve the mystery of the vanished flight 370.

* Thirdly, the saving of fuel is a factor. Plus, the factor of fuel consumption can become critical after daily aerial searching is completed, when it becomes time to return hundreds of miles back to the Australian airbase for refueling, maintenance, and human searcher solid sleep.

PART 15

DAY no. 22, Friday, March 28, 2014 (EST), finds Wolf Blitzer convening a panel of experts that include scientists, oceanographers, and hydrologists. Mr. Rob McCallum, a professional expedition leader, points out that the Deepwater Situated Wreckage is beneficial to the on-going Boeing-777 search because:

1) Water carries sound waves both excellently and distantly. ("Black boxes" emit an audio ping.)
2) Deepwater is preferable because of the greater silence, thereby making it easier to detect and hear quiet pinging, should/or, if both "black box" batteries have either diminished and/or degraded in electrical power.

Mr. Keith Masback, CEO of US Geo-Spatial Intelligence Foundation and an expert in geo-spatial searching abilities, with expertise in satellite observation, as well as, aerial reconnaissance and searching, reminds interested individuals that thirteen years ago: a United States P-3 aircraft collided with a Chinese aircraft (probably within Chinese borders), thereby allowing the Chinese to examine the US P-3, and then, reverse-engineer the advanced features of the US P-3, to build A Chinese version of the United States P-3.

But why capture a Boeing-777, when a buyer can purchase one from Boeing company?

Dr. Sanjay Gupta, neurosurgeon, delivers a pre-diagnosis/prognosis view on the physical strain caused to the surviving family members, of the missing 239 passengers and crew, who probably all are experiencing the following:

1) Increased stress levels,
2) Hypertension (elevated blood pressure),
3) Raised cortisone levels that may never return to normal,
4) Psychological impact of grieving the loss of a loved one, and the obtaining of a sense of closure to the disaster of a possible crashing of the MA flight no. MH-370, leading to either a missing or possible deceased relative,
5) And hopefully, as the entire world observes the MH-370 calamity and joins together, in a fact-finding search to explain the fate of missing flight 370, that a factual explanation can lead to, gleaning a sense of closure.

Later, on day no. 22, Wolf Blitzer invites a three-person expert panel composed of the following:

A) Mr. Mark Weiss, retired B-777 pilot;
B) Mr. Peter Goelz, former NTSB managing director;
C) Mr. Tom Fuentes, former FBI chief investigator.

Curious persons email questions, needing answers, to these three experts:

1) Buoys are being placed, not only to mark the Flotsam spotted but also to track the movement of the Indian Ocean currents.
2) Each country participating in the search for wreckage are covering their own expenses. However, in about three more weeks, a reassessment of costs may be billed to certain countries.
3) Background checks on the crew, including both pilots as well as all the stewards and/or stewardesses have been conducted, leading to finding no evidence connecting any of

them to the missing Malaysia Airlines flight 370. And very contentiously controversial is MH-370's Captain Shah's, at-home and hand-built flight simulator!

However, *after* the completion of investigator's examinations, the flight simulator *is not* revealing any connection whatsoever to the missing Boeing-777, known as flight 370. But what is revealed is Boeing manufacturing company's patent on technology permitting an aircraft to be flown and controlled from the ground in a drone-like fashion.

Plus: more background checks of the two passengers holding two stolen passports have indicated no foul play, at least so far.

In addition, the daughter of the missing Captain Shah, chief pilot, who was flying the missing Boeing-777 rejects allegations made by England's Daily Mirror Publication, insisting her father did nothing untoward, in the plight of vanished MA flight no. MH-370.

PART 16

In a forty-eight-hour time period, encompassing days no. 23 and no. 24, Saturday and Sunday, March 29 and March 30, 2014 (EST), as multiple eleven search aircraft and ten search ships continue to scour the latest potential "debris field," nothing more, aviation-related, has been located in the search for flight no. MH-370, a Boeing-777.

Compassion should be shared with the 239 missing passenger's and crew's surviving families' members and friends, but as well, with all those brave humanitarians, risking all their lives on the dangerous ocean, whether in search aircraft and/or search ships, during almost three and one-half weeks of daily searching, to rescue and/or recover 239 people or victims.

Recovery of the missing B-777 will furnish the answers to: Why? How? Where? When? The Earths' populace needs to know facts and evidence!

PART 17

It is now Monday, March 31, 2014 (EST), and day no. 25 since flight no. MH-370 disappeared. The *Wall Street Journal* (WSJ) is circulating this fact: (Quote) "Poor communication between countries, led to three days of searching in the wrong area" (end of WSJ quote). Most agree the country of Malaysia has furnished conflicting information and viewpoints. Ms. Sara Sidner, CNN correspondent, is reporting to Wolf Blitzer from Kuala Lumpur, Malaysia, that the surviving families' members, of the missing 239 passengers and crew, are unhappy with the type of investigation being done by the Malaysian government. One day, the Malaysian prime minister announces, "No survivors on missing flight no. MH-370." Yet the Malaysian minister of transportation says otherwise. Simply, that the flight of MA no. MH-370 ended on the Indian Ocean. Many of the surviving families' members prefer the notion of a hi-jacking to compare to a crash. Some hold hope that passengers are alive.

Mr. David Funk, retired Northwest Airlines pilot, speaking to anchorman Jake Tapper, says Malaysia is not up to date on accident investigation, as well as the sharing of aircraft accident data. And Miles O'Brien tells Anderson Cooper that Malaysia has been relatively silent in the releasing of important information, because of the rivalry, among adjacent countries in the region, including militarily.

For example, originally the Malaysia governmental investigators released a statement claiming the last and final radio communication, between flight no. MH-370 signing off with the Kuala Lumpur International Airport control tower, made flying above the South China Sea was "Good night, Malaysia 370".

In reality, thanks to world pressure for actual facts, information, and details: It was then later revealed, from the control tower taping of radio communications with flight no. MH-370, that what was really spoken by Captain Shah (during the final sign off to the Kuala Lumpur International Airport Control Tower) was "Goodnight Malaysia 3-7-0", while flying the Boeing-777 north, northeast (NNE) above the South China Sea before turning left (port) (to fly west).

Ms. Mary Schiavo, former head of accident investigation of the DOT (US Department of Transportation) says, "This Is a Normal Aircraft Comment" (probably referencing each and both versions of communication sign off).

Still, each version is different!

Mr. Anderson Cooper then inquires of US Navy commander William Marks, stationed on the US Navy's command ship *Blue Ridge*, on the reliability of American search equipment, whether airborne or search-ship based. In reply, Commander Marks states the US Navy's *Blue Ridge* can sight small objects of potential aircraft wreckage. Also, the *Blue Ridge* carries a US "towed pinger locator" (TPL), plus an underwater and unmanned "autonomous underwater vehicle" (AUV) with side-scan radar. Unfortunately, the *Blue Ridge* US search ship will face a delay, in its travel from the United States to the southern Indian Ocean because of the prerequisite retro-fitting necessary to launch both the "towed pinger locator" (TPL) as well as the "autonomous underwater vehicle" (AUV). (Mr. David Gallo, Woods-Hole Oceanographic Institute's AUV expert and oceanographer will soon explain.)

Also, the Australians are ramping up search efforts. Mr. Will Ripley is reporting Australia is dispatching its *Ocean Shield* search ship to the search area. The *Ocean Shield* will be capable of towing the US Navy's "TPL" (towed pinger locator), which can detect the once-per-second "black boxes" audio pings, emitted from both "black boxes" ping beacons.

To receive a good, clear audio ping signal, the "TPL" prefers an over-beacon position or within a one-mile beacon horizontal range.

Vertically, the "TPL" is listening in the deep water, of the Indian Ocean sea-floor search area.

A possible depth of twenty thousand feet or three to four miles deep, may be encountered. This difficult task may be mitigated by the discovery of floating Boeing-777 debris. Aircraft debris or wreckage Flotsam found, speeds up the "TPL" detecting task of locating the position of the two "black boxes," and their flight 370 physical Boeing-777.

Mr. David Gallo says, once pin-pointed, deep diving unmanned, autonomous underwater vehicles (AUVs), equipped with robotic manipulators (mechanical hands) capable of object-grasping, can begin the recovery of actual physical Boeing-777 evidence. If not precisely pin-pointed by the "TPL," then, the autonomous underwater vehicle (AUV) would dive near the sea floor of the search zone. Its side-scan radar, combing the sea floor is capable of identifying a sunken aircraft or its components, e.g., an aircraft wing or main landing gear or its tail section, etc.

United States secretary of defense, Mr. Chuck Hagel is stating, to Ms. Brooke Baldwin, that the US and Australia are doing all possible to locate missing flight 370, including increasing search assets in terms of search aircraft and search ships.

The Australian *Ocean Shield* search ship is racing to the latest search area, as indicated by the Inmarsat satellite data, but will take two more days to arrive, considering the vast expanse of the Indian Ocean. And flight 370 is felt to have ditched distantly from Australia's western coastline. The new search area (as indicated by the Inmarsat satellite analytical data) is a very large one hundred thousand–square mile area. Miles O'Brien, Peter Goelz, Richard Quest, and Tom Fuentes, all express concern, as to the question of the many search aircraft and search ships, looking in the most fruitful area of the new search zone that might, indeed yield Boeing-777 debris.

Time is running short. The time constraints are the following:

A) Twenty-five days have elapsed without any trace of actual Boeing-777 wreckage, or any debris.

B) The "TPL" (towed pinger locator) must spend days to canvass a fruitful zone that might detect the audio pings emitted from the "black box(es)" beacon(s).

C) And the "black box(es)"—ping emitting, beacon(s)' batteries may only have five days of electrical charge remaining, based on a thirty-day life span of charge. With luck, should the charge in the two "black box" batteries last up to forty days, then a weakened pinging might still be heard by the "TPL." Plus, the "TPL" locates better with two direct overhead passes.

D) The Australian search ship *Ocean Shield*, needing two days to arrive on scene, would then only have three days of towing the "TPL," if the "black box"—audio ping emitting, beacon's batteries do have a thirty-day electrical charge, assuming they were properly stored and maintained.

E) Aircraft, in the maintenance hangar, undergo much preventative maintenance, ranging from light service to heavy dismantling and rebuild, known as A-check, B-check, C-check, and D-check. If flight 370's last C-check was properly executed, according to the Manufacturer's Maintenance Manual (the aircraft's Bible), then the chances are better improved for a thirty- to forty-day beacon battery life.

Regarding *The Wall Street Journal*'s quote of "Poor communication between countries led to three days of searching in the wrong area," Malaysian civilians, unhappy with the type of investigation being done by the Malaysia government (see page 50), have made their own new map showing an alternate flight path by missing flight no. MH-370. Interestingly, this map is indicative of a skilled pilot at the cockpit controls. But Malaysia authorities cite this new flight path would constitute a criminal act.

However, Miles O'Brien contends this new flight path could have been accomplished by virtually anyone having some piloting experience and engaging the Boeing-777's automatic pilot computer, by programming in new way points. "Way points" for aircraft, may be comparatively synonymous with street signs and/or intersections for automobiles, using regularly traveled routes.

And regarding the new one hundred thousand square mile search area based on Inmarsat analytical data (see page 52), Brooke Baldwin interviews Mr. Tim Taylor, of Tiburon Subs Company (submarines). Tim Taylor, an underwater search equipment expert with Tiburon sub(mersible)s company, says locating A "black box" within a one hundred thousand–square mile area is a difficult undertaking. Tim states that just a cursory search of a ten thousand–square mile area would take two years to complete. A more detailed underwater search, featuring excellent imaging, could take a period of time elapsing two to six years to complete.

Mr. Tim Taylor, after mathematically describing the ratios of numbers involved in the search to locate flight no. MH-370 goes on to mention all this could dwarf enormously the search for still-missing-aviatrix Ms. Amelia Earhart! Should the search (for MH-370) exceed one hundred years and surpass billions of dollars spent, the end result could be 239 people never being found!

Mr. Kit Darby, a former United Airlines pilot and president of kitdarby.com (aviation consulting), tells Wolf Blitzer, the Boeing-777 is very well-built and is the favored choice of most pilots around the world they would pick to fly. Kit also agrees with the Thai(land) radar sighting, and by factoring in the rate of fuel burn at a decreased altitude of twelve thousand feet, the new search location is probably the most mathematically correct area, for the vanished flight 370 to have possibly ditched.

Now Brooke Baldwin questions Mr. William J. McGee, author of his book answering the eight chief reasons for aircraft accidents. Brooke asks William about the upgrading of human flight, from twentieth century "black box" technology to twenty-first century direct air-to-ground data feed technology? (And/or air to satellite to ground). Mr. McGee responds (as many others have), airlines are always weighing cost(s) versus the safety of passengers (and people on the ground), and that cost(s) usually wins out in the blocking of aircraft safety upgrades, due to the high expense(s), needed to be spent, to implement new electronic communications (air to ground to air), while, simultaneously, not interrupting the tens of thousands of daily flights all year. Yet such advanced twenty-first century technology exists.

Regarding aviation technological upgrading versus cost(s), faced by airline companies: Miles O'Brien and Michael Goldfarb, both speaking with Jake Tapper, revealed the fact that Malaysia Airlines Company did not, spend the additional ten dollars per passenger per flight to upgrade the ACAR/ACART safety system on their entire fleet of aircraft at/or owned by Malaysia Airlines Company! So costs seem to impede the speedy implementation of safety advances on many aircraft, as well as competing airline companies, internationally.

In the United States, the Federal Aviation Administration (FAA), overseen by the US Department of Transportation (DOT), requires American Airline Companies to have and use the upgraded ACAR/ACART system. Internationally, other airline companies also utilize the upgraded ACAR/ACART system. (See pages 31 and 32.)

At the end of today, day no. 25, eleven search aircraft and ten search ships have not yet found floating Boeing-777 wreckage. Because the basic law of hydraulics states liquids behave as solids, an aircraft nose-diving into the Indian Ocean at high speed would smash apart, similar to striking concrete (causing aircraft wreckage and/or debris Flotsam to form).

Perhaps flight 370, horizontally glided onto the Indian Ocean surface and sank intact!

PART 18

It has now become day no. 26, Tuesday, April 1, 2014 (EST), and Brooke Baldwin is conversing with Chad Myers. Chad says we know little about our Earth's oceans. To map our Earth's oceans' sea floors, in totality, would require an effort exceeding a duration of 2,900 years! In reality, we (Earthlings) know more about the Martian surface (another planet) and the size and depth of the craters on our Earth's moon!

Fortunately, the deep water(s) of the Indian Ocean may be advantageous, for the task of the "TPL" to detect and hear the once per second audio pingings emitted by the "black boxes" battery-operated beacons:

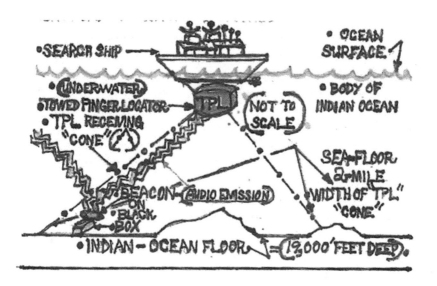

In addition, luckily, it is a scientific fact that sound travels five times more efficiently and effectively underwater (or within a liquid), than sound travels atmospherically (or through air).

The proper tow speed of the Australian search ship *Ocean Shield*, while towing the US built "TPL" underwater will be about five knots per hour equaling five to six miles per hour (MPH).

Mr. Bill Schofield, a technologist who worked on the concept of and the building of the first aviation "black boxes," and speaking with Ms. Erin Burnett, states the batteries on the "black boxes," on-board vanished flight no. MH-370, are soon to diminish and therefore degrade. Bill says, "It would be easier to find a needle in a haystack."

Earlier today, Mr. Jim Sciutto discussed the topic of flight 370's fuel range with Mr. Miles O'Brien, a pilot and PBS's chief science correspondent. Miles replied by delivering a technical and mathematical explanation, as to why the missing Boeing-777 possibly might not have made it to the current search zone, presently being examined by eleven search aircraft and nine search ships.

[And now joining in this extraordinary search is the HMS *Tireless*, a British nuclear-powered submarine first class, having sonar, side-scan radar, and capable of diving easily to depths of twenty thousand feet.]

Mr. O'Brien is pointing (verbally), to the relationship of fuel consumption to distance flown, being affected, by the factoring in of flight 370's altitude and its engines revolutions per minute (RPM) (normally increased to climb, overcoming the opposite force of gravity, for instance). And weather is always a prevalent ramification of flight. Various radars have placed flight 370 flying at various altitudes, ranging from a lofty forty-five thousand feet, down to a low (oxygen-breathable) twelve thousand feet. Denser air at twelve thousand feet = greater drag = greater RPM = greater fuel consumption!

Ms. Kyung Lau, reporting from Perth, Australia (and in contact with Wolf Blitzer), says the eleven search aircraft, about to take off, will now be accompanied by an air traffic control airplane to assist in the prevention of collision(s) between close proximity aircraft, as all on-board tend to be head down bent, searching for any trace of a vanished Boeing-777, transporting 239 passengers and crew, now missing twenty-six days.

Miles O'Brien adds, the written transcription of communications, between flight no. MH-370 and the Kuala Lumpur International Airport control tower is not enough.

The verbal communications of an audio-taping format is much preferred because it provides more in that analysis of voices can reveal voice stresses, plus background sounds, such as the noise(s) of a cockpit security door opening and closing, and those voices in conversation, such as radio communications, pilot communications, and also, warning bells and buzzers. And what about an unknown third voice intrusively?

Earlier today, Mr. Marcus Eriksen, ocean pollution expert and executive director of The Five Gyres Institute, told Brooke Baldwin that he has visited all five of our Earth's gyres:

1) The Indian Ocean Gyre
2) The South Pacific Ocean Gyre
3) The North Pacific Ocean Gyre
4) The North Atlantic Ocean Gyre
5) The South Atlantic Ocean Gyre

Marcus, also an oceanographer, explains that much of the satellite-sighted ocean surface debris is plastic(s) in origin. Plastic(s) can have a life span of hundreds of years, before totally deteriorating by ultraviolet rays of sunlight, and he says that we need to clean our oceans.

This plastic debris may be obscuring the viewing of fragmentary Boeing-777 wreckage!

Bill Schofield (see page 57), "black box" innovator, in agreement with William J. McGee (see page 55), claims that a satellite uplink methodology to replace the twentieth century "black box" technology, would be paid for by increased costs passed on to the flying public.

So at the end of the day (no. 26), Ms. Renee Marsh, aviation consultant and analyst, sadly, reports on the possibility of missing flight no. MH-370 *never again being found!* In response to Renee, a former NTSB (US National Transportation Safety Board) official replies that aviation needs facts that make scientific sense, in order to correct the problems found, whether electrical, meteorological, electronic, mechanical, etc., that may be why MH-370 vanished.

However, if the vanished aircraft is never found, then, the aviation industry will not satisfactorily advance into the future of the remaining twenty-first century, in that, without answers from physical evidence, the tragic incident of missing MA flight no. MH-370 may possibly be repeated, leading to the loss of another two to three hundred paying passengers of the flying public!

PART 19

It is now the next day, Wednesday, April 2, 2014 (EST), and day no. 27 of the vanished Boeing-777 200 series (model, type). All 227 missing passengers have now been cleared of foul play, involving the disappearance of Malaysia Airlines flight no. MH-370, according to Ms. Carol Costello, CNN anchorwoman. This official clearance was granted by the investigation conducted by the Malaysian government. Mr. Tom Fuentes, former FBI assistant director and chief investigator, now retired, states the official clearance from foul play, granted by the Malaysian government's investigation of the 227 missing passengers, is relying on all the police interviews and detective work executed by the authorities of those countries the passengers were citizens of.

Now the focus of the Malaysian's government investigation has narrowed down to the two crew members, assigned to flying fight 370 by their joint and/or individual operation(s), inside the flight cabin (cockpit): Captain Zahari Shah, commanding from the L/H (left-hand) seat, and his first officer (co-pilot), Fariq Hamid, working from the R/H (right-hand) seat. Flight 370s ten flight attendants' responsibilities in the passenger cabin are to assist the 227 passengers, by providing safety measures, and comfort variables (creature comforts).

Due to the Malaysian government's investigation now examining the operation(s) performed by the two-person flight crew, from within the cockpit of disappeared flight 370, Mr. Martin Savidge, CNN correspondent, is now reporting from within a Boeing-777 flight simulator, along with Mr. Mitchell Casado, pilot instructor/trainer. Together, they are demonstrating how the entry door to the flight cabin has been strengthened, reinforced, and buttressed, to prevent illicit entry(ies) by an unauthorized intruder(s) (since the twin tower tragedy which occurred thirteen years ago on September 11, 2001). The redesigned entry door, now implemented on all Boeing-777s (and many other aircraft in the aftermath of the September 11, 2001 catastrophies), features additional anti-access measures, including,

A) An electric/electronic locking mechanism;
B) Another actual manually-operated deadbolt;
C) Plus, new training involving the entire crew, including flight attendants who may physically enter the flight cabin (in the event of an exiting pilot temporarily using the facilities), to provide assistance with the remaining pilot in controlling the flight of the aircraft, while other flight attendants simultaneously bodily block access to the outer door handle, in a group display of potential physical force, even utilizing a beverage cart for blocking an approaching threat to flight-cabin security.

Meanwhile, the Australian search ship *Ocean Shield* is now one day away from "steaming" into the latest search field, as one dozen search aircraft and nine search ships, plus a British nuclear-powered submarine, HMS *The Tireless*, continue to scour the Indian Ocean, as indicated by the presently most reliable and accurate data, provided by the Inmarsat satellite's six and one-half "handshake(s) communications" with flight 370, and radar-blips of its flight path.

As Malaysia is, more and more, requesting greater United States assistance with search equipment and aviation disaster advice, US secretary of defense, Mr. Chuck Hagel, is now en route to meet with the Malaysian chief investigator in Hawaii (a middle ground area in distance between Kuala Lumpur, Malaysia, and Washington, DC). Ms. Mary Schiavo, opining to Carol Costello, thinks her gut feeling, stemming from her immense aviation accident investigation and experience(s), says flight 370 vanished due to the following:

1) A catastrophic event occurred suddenly, and
2) Inadequate crew training, in reaction to respond to properly address such sudden catastrophic event, which may have occurred.

The Earth's population, after twenty-seven days of a large, wide-bodied Boeing-777 vanishing without a trace of tangible, physical evidence, wonders what caused its disappearance, and *how, where, and why?*

Rob McCallum wonders also. Without the discovery of floating B-777 aircraft wreckage, Rob is suggesting beginning sonar exploration. Could search ship sonar from the ocean's surface and submarine sonar by the on-scene HMS *The Tireless* (all done before, the battery-operated black box audio ping emitting beacons go silent), yield results?

So does the official investigation of the Malaysian government. As their focus narrows, they are inspecting closely the food prepared for the two pilots (their menu being different than the passengers menu). Also, which menu was offered the passengers? Could this mean suspicion of poisoning food?

And so do two CNN correspondents, Ms. Paula Stewart and Ms. Christine Dennison, who are reporting to Ms. Ashleigh Banfield. They both agree, for the aerial and/or search-ship inspection to be fruitful, the latest search field needs to be reduced 1,000 percent, basically from a one hundred thousand square mile search area to a one hundred square mile search area, according to their sources.

And Will Ripley, based in Australia, is also in agreement with the mathematical ratio reduction of 1,000 percent, according to his sources for facts. Interestingly, Wolf Blitzer, in contact with other ocean-search experts, is now stating there is a new prime search zone located two hundred miles east of the preexisting search field, placing it only 926 miles west of Perth, Australia.

Wolf's next Expert Guest, Mr. Arnold Carr, concerned with the remaining strength in the black box electrically, battery-powered, once per second, audio ping emitting beacons(s), is suggesting a yet closer analysis, of the existing, scientifically-factual radar(s)' "blip" information/data, to more precisely pinpoint the location of missing flight 370.

Regarding a closer analysis of the factual radar "blip" data, David Soucie states a new and clever ideation. David is suggesting the best untried method to locate missing MA flight 370, is for an identical aircraft (namely a Boeing-777-200 series), to re-fly the exact flight path of flight 370, according to scientifically reliable and factually exact, existing radar data, to pinpoint a much more precise, possible, aircraft ocean-ditching site.

Of course the re-fly aircraft must replicate, and contain the identical fuel quantity, as well as an equivalent weight load, as the 239 victims possessed, replete with cargo weight of all luggage and other baggage items loaded into the cargo compartment(s) of missing flight 370, the night it vanished.

This is easily done with iron weight, and is extremely relevant, in that, all pilots, prior to take-off and flight, must mathematically calculate three vital factors:

1) Weight of aircraft when completely empty,
2) Weight of fuel quantity (aircraft fuel quantity gauges display pounds of fuel),
3) Weight of cargo, plus exact passenger count (including crew members).

The above factors equal total weight, and flight safety is reliant on total weight:

A) Main runway length (for safe take off),
B) Flight range safety (destination distance),

C) Landing aircraft weight (fuel quantity is reduced at destination site),

D) Emergency landing weight (runway length and fuel quantity become major factors).

Note: In the global aviation industry (both civil and commercial), any emergency landing is defined as "a good landing," when 100 percent of all the passengers and crew survive deplaning, and better still, emerge unscathed (including ground population).

Regarding re-fly test flight advantage(s), David Soucie now tells Ms. Deborah Feyerick, CNN correspondent, search aircraft may then sight floating Boeing-777 aircraft debris from an ocean-surface impact. Search ships then can recover and verify authenticity. Should the identification be positive, then *Ocean Shield* can tow The "TPL" over a potentially fruitful search site, leading to finding the two "black boxes," and possibly the entire B-777 aircraft wreckage. Then, the possibility of the recovery of victims, "black boxes," and pieces of B-777 may be accomplished using AUVs having manipulators, floatation air bags, and possibly, ship-mounted heavy-lift cranes.

Because an aircraft's transponder is under the manual control of both pilots in the flight-cabin for safety and/or emergency reasons, according to Boeing-777 pilot Mark Weiss, Wolf Blitzer introduces Miles O'Brien, pilot and aviation analyst. Miles is telling Wolf, Malaysia Airlines has now adopted and implemented a policy that has been in effect since the September 11, 2001, catastrophies here in the United States. This policy, new to Malaysia Airlines, states, "Never leave a single individual alone in the cockpit!" Rather, nowadays, if one member of the flight crew exits the flight cabin (cockpit), it is now incumbent on another authorized aircraft support employee, to enter the cockpit (effectively keeping a second person within the confines of the flight cabin), whether it be a navigator, a flight attendant, or some authorized employee of that particular flight, so as to then, avoid having a single person in complete control of the aircraft-in-flight, with the high-security entry door closed, locked, and bolted shut, until the original crew member (who left the flight cabin, cockpit), returns to his/her designated position within the flight cabin.

Then, the high-security cockpit entry door, again, is closed, locked, and bolted shut. However, twenty-seven days ago, Malaysia Airlines had not yet adopted and implemented this particular policy of cockpit regulation. Does this indicate the chance, twenty-seven days ago, of a singular pilot, or third person, turning off the transponder, and intentionally, or vicariously, hi-jacking flight 370 for yet-unknown nefarious purposes?

Again, the profundity of the mystery of flight 370's disappearance seems to deepen further and farther into the darkness of uncertainty!

Earlier today, Wolf Blitzer announced the moving of the search area two hundred miles east (see page 63), to a new location sited 926 miles west of Perth, Australia. Now, later tonight, Mr. Mathew Chance, reporting during the Don Lemon newscast, states the newest search field is 1,031 miles west of the western coast of Australia. Perhaps, assuming both descriptions are accurate, they jointly delineate a "search box", having both an eastern and western boundary, 105 miles wide. (See pages 62 and 63.)

Meanwhile (also today), a press conference is being held in Australia, involving two prime ministers (PMs), Australian PM Mr. Tony Abbott and Malaysian PM Mr. Najib Razak.

PART 20

N ow it is day no. 28, Thursday, April 3, 2014 (EST = EDT), and also four weeks since MA flight no. MH-370 disappeared. Still, *no trace of physical evidence!* Additionally, at yesterday's Australian press conference, both prime ministers, Tony Abbott, Australian PM, and Najib Razak, Malaysian PM, applauded the united cooperation of greater than seven nations actively participating in the search for missing Malaysia Airlines flight no. MH-370, including the following:

* Malaysia
* China (who have Chinese nationals in excess of 50 percent of MH-370's passenger manifest)
* Australia (providing the search ship *Ocean Shield*)
* The United States (who is providing both the "TPL" and the "AUV")
* The United Kingdom (who is providing the nuclear-powered submarine HMS *The Tireless*)
* Japan
* New Zealand

And greater beyond than these listed seven nations are providing, altogether, ten search aircraft and nine to twelve search ships, all probing and seeking daily, B-777 wreckage.

Note: Daylight savings time has already commenced. Hence, time references noted as Eastern Standard Time (EST) become known as Eastern Daylight Time (EDT), during the summer season of our Earth's northern hemisphere. Simultaneously, our Earth's southern hemisphere experiences winter. The ongoing search for vanished flight no. MH-370, at the south fortieth degree of latitude, is winter.

So at the beginning of today, day no. 28, at 12:07 AM (EDT), Mr. Don Lemon is hosting five expert guests. Don's panel of aviation analysts consists of Mr. Jim Tilmon, retired pilot, Mr. Les Abend, active Boeing-777 pilot, Mr. David Soucie, author of *Why Planes Crash*, Mr. Michael Kay, British RAF pilot and mathematician, and Mr. Jeff Wise, author of *Extreme Fear*. Michael suggests searching farther north, in the Northern Indian Ocean.

Later, near the end of today, day no. 28, at 11:20 PM (EDT), another important news conference is occurring in Perth, Australia. Simultaneously, in Perth, Australia, their time zone is twelve hours earlier, or 11:20 AM (EDT) of Friday morning on April 4, 2014. This important news conference is headed by Mr. Angus Houston (chief air marshall, retired), who is the present head (leader) of Australia's joint agency search for MA flight no. MH-370. During this news conference, Angus Houston announced the deploying of the underwater search assets (from Australia's *Ocean Shield*):

1) Now: The US Navy's "TPL" (towed pinger locator),
2) Later: The US-built AUV (autonomous underwater vehicle) named *Bluefin-21*.

Angus also states, both the aircraft search as well as the search ships will continue their ongoing reconnaissance, hoping to locate verifiable Boeing-777 aircraft Flotsam.

PART 21

D ay no. 29 is Friday, April 4, 2014 (EDT of EST). Brooke Baldwin (while introducing Angus Houston, retired chief air marshall), is saying, "The search which Mr. Angus Houston is in charge of is science and speculation". It should be pointed out, that, while Malaysia remains the lead chief of the investigation in the disappearance of MA flight no. MH-370, Malaysia has officially transferred all searching operations and those responsibilities entailed to Australia, under the leadership of Mr. Angus Houston, whether above or below the surface of the Indian Ocean. All based on the available, reliable, and accurate data. (From radar(s) and Inmarsat satellite(s)).

So today, day no. 29, Angus Houston is in charge of the US-built "TPL" (see page 56), which he deployed beginning today, Friday, April 4, 2014 (EDT), from (and being towed by), the Australian search ship *Ocean Shield*, as well as all aerial search and search ship observatory assets, that continue in their dedicated wreckage search for identifiable Boeing-777 components.

Meanwhile, inside the Boeing-777 flight simulator, Martin Savidge and pilot instructor Mitchell Casada are demonstrating how the highly designed and advanced glide characteristics, engineered by Boeing aircraft manufacturing company into their model-777 aircraft, may/can allow, possibly, for a smooth contact and entry onto/ into the Indian Ocean.

This means it is possible the entire Boeing-777 (or most of it), may have submerged virtually intact to the sea floor of the Indian Ocean! However, SCUBA (self-contained underwater breathing apparatus) divers, cannot dive and work in the deep waters of the Indian Ocean. The sea floors in the search area(s) of this portion of the Indian Ocean are as deep as three to four miles; fifteen thousand to twenty thousand feet. Therefore, recovery efforts will need to be handled robotically, using "TPLs" and "AUVs". These are "towed pinger locators" and "autonomous underwater vehicles"; all, of course, are unmanned and controlled by ocean surface search ships. (See page 56.)

Pressurization underwater is measured in increments named "atmospheres." At sea level, the pressure of air is 14.7 pounds per square inch (ten Newtons per square centimeter). People do not implode (crush) from this external force of one atmosphere (14.7 pounds per square inch), because, internally, every cell of the human body is oxygenated to one atmosphere, thereby counterbalancing both external and internal pressures to equalization. Each thirty-three feet of depth underwater equals one atmosphere of external pressure (caused by the enormous weight of water).

PART 22

Now, it is Saturday, April 5, 2014 (EDT), and day no. 30 since flight no. MH-370 departed Kuala Lumpur International Airport, flew, and *disappeared!* Today, at noontime, a Chinese search ship has heard and located an underwater "audio pinging" sound, at a frequency of 37.5 KHZ!

The two "black boxes," on-board the vanished Boeing-777-200 MA flight no. MH-370, have "once per second, audio ping emitting, battery-powered, transmitting beacon(s)." These two B-777 "black box" beacons transmit "audio pings," at a frequency of 37.5 KHZ.

The "TPL" (towed pinger locator) is a "receiver," capable of hearing the audio pingings transmitted from the "black box" beacons and determining their frequency, while totally immersed underwater. When the "TPL" registers an incoming audio pinging (at the rate of one per second), transmitted at the frequency of 37.5 KHZ, it has heard the black box's beacon.

Plus, the entire aircraft may be nearby, hopefully!

The Chinese search ship used a primitive hand-held microphone, that was held three feet, beneath the Indian Ocean surface. It was detected southeast (SE) of the three previous and currently active searching sites. Afterward, a Chinese search aircraft overflew the area of the 37.5 KHZ ping detection (that was heard earlier today for one and one-half minutes). It spotted several floating objects, white-in-color, on the ocean surface over the area of pinging (at 37.5 KHZ for one and a half minutes).

Eleven hours later, still during day no. 30, Angus Houston is now reporting, that Australia's *Ocean Shield* search ship has now towed the US Navy's "TPL," over a second "pinging" site, (first for the TPL), in the area of their latest search zone. This second "audio pinging" detected (first for the TPL), is in the vicinity of the southern "arc," where the Inmarsat Satellite Co.'s scientists mathematically determined to be where, the six and one-half "handshake" communications, last received from missing flight 370, occurred. This second "pinging" (the first detected by *Ocean Shield*'s TPL), is being emitted from a "beacon" located at a depth of fourteen thousand feet–plus.

The *Ocean Shield* next will steam to the area of the Chinese audio pinging detection to verify the frequency emitted, with the US "TPL."

PART 23

Sunday, April 6, 2014 (EDT), becomes day no. 31 of the disappearance of Malaysia Airlines flight no. MH-370. Luckily, weather conditions are good, yesterday and today (days no. 30 and no. 31), in both Indian Ocean search areas, allowing both aircraft and surface ship surveillances(s) to continue unaffected and unimpeded. This is according to Ms. Jennifer Gray, CNN meteorologist, as she speaks with Ms. Fredrika Whitfield, CNN anchorwoman, about her weather forecast, mentioning the formation of a new cyclone (hurricane), yesterday, Saturday, April 5, 2014 (EDT), distantly west of the ongoing rescue/recovery mission.

Today, day no. 31, Don Lemon, consulting with his expert panel consisting of Les Abend, active Boeing-777 pilot, Mr. Don Ginzburg, audio sciences expert, and Richard Quest, aviation analyst, asks about the importance of installing interior cockpit cameras having the ability to stream live images to dedicated orbiting satellites, possessing sufficient memory, to digitally record the interior cockpit camers(s) imagery transmitted?

Les Abend replies with answers revealing/containing a relevant caveat. Namely, the pilot(s), judgmentally, must have master control of the cockpit camera circuitry, enabling those pilots dealing with fire or other emergency, to switch them off.

PART 24

DAY no. 32 is Monday, April 7, 2014 (US EDT), when, beginning at midnight, 12:00 AM to 1:00 AM (EDT), a news conference from Perth, Australia, is being held by Chief Air Marshall Angus Houston (Ret.). (The time zone in Perth, Australia, is twelve hours earlier: 12:00 PM noontime to 1:00 PM, Monday, day no. 32). Angus clarifies the following:

A) The Australian search ship *Ocean Shield*, towing the US-built "TPL" (towed pinger locator), underwater, has confirmed an "audio pinging," detected and heard yesterday, Sunday, April 6, 2014, is being emitted from a depth of 4,500 meters below the Indian Ocean surface. This "TPL" is provided by Phoenix International Company in the State of Maryland, United States.

B) A second distinct "audio pinging" was also detected and heard on Sunday, April 6, 2014, by *Ocean Shield*'s TPL, and also emanated from a depth of 4,500 meters.

C) Both "audio pingings" transmitted from two separate beacons at a frequency of 37.5 KHZ, and at one-ping-per-second time intervals, are consistent with known "black box beacon" transmitting parameters.

D) 1. The first "audio pinging" detected by *Ocean Shield*'s towed pinger locator (TPL), was heard at a distance of 1,800 yards away from the second audio pingings' detection. This is importantly relevant because:

D) 2. The first audio pinging heard, lasted a time duration of two hours and twenty minutes. Could the first audio pinging have been transmitted from the flight data recorders (FDR's) beacon?

D) 3. The other, second audio pinging heard, lasted a time duration of thirteen minutes. Could the second audio pinging have been transmitted from the cockpit voice recorder's (CVR's) beacon?

E) Yesterday, Sunday, April 6, 2014, the *Ocean Shield's* TPL steamed over and confirmed the audio pinging detected by the Chinese search ship's hand-held submersible microphone on Saturday, April 5, 2014, as also being located at a depth of 4,500 meters, as well, below the Indian Ocean's surface.

Two search ships (one Chinese, one Australian), have detected and heard a total of three separate "audio pinging transmissions," all tuned to 37.5 KHZ. The Chinese audio pinging was one incidence. And the Australian audio pinging detections were two incidences. All three at 4,500 meters deep: 4,500 meters = 2.8 miles = 14,764 feet. Angus Houston says 4,500 meters is extremely deep.

Phoenix international company's "TPL" can operate at a depth of twenty thousand feet. It is towed as low as one mile above the sea floor, while its "receiver" scans a two-mile wide "cone." This two-mile wide "cone of reception" is illustrated on page 56.

However, Phoenix International Co.'s "AUV" (autonomous underwater vehicle), named *Bluefin-21*, is designed and built to operate safely, between depths in the ocean ranging, from thirteen thousand feet to 14,900 feet, and possibly twenty thousand feet. Below twenty thousand feet, the risk of implosion becomes a reality, by exceeding too many atmospheres of severe pressure(s). (See page 69.) Twenty thousand feet of depth = 606.06 atmospheres. 606.06 atmospheres × 14.7 pounds per inch (air pressure at sea level) = 8,908.2 pounds per square inch of pressure (at twenty thousand feet of depth)!

Fortunately, the AUV *Bluefin-21* easily can operate at an ocean depth of 4,500 meters. 4,500 meters = 14,763.78 feet of depth.

And its photographic, as well as, side-scan radar(s) will map the sea-floor in the prime search zone where audio pinging was heard. The side scan radar system can distinguish between the natural form of the sea floor as compared to the man-made shaping of an aircraft. Particularly, objects having square or rectangular dimensions, main landing gear design (with their perfectly round tires), and the unique shape of an aircraft tail section assembly, etc.

Agreeing with Angus Houston is Commander William Marks, on board the USS *Blue Ridge*, United States Navy's seventh fleet, confirming that the pinging emitted and heard at one-second time intervals is consistent with black box beacon pinging emissions(s). Furthermore, William says the two "black boxes" can be located by utilizing "triangulation." "Triangulation" is a mathematical calculus proven by science to pinpoint a particular objective. This triangulation is accomplished by making three lines of passes with the search ship towing the "TPL" over the "pinging site." Where these three lines intersect indicates precisely the location of the object emitting the audio pinging detected and heard.

Regarding "pinging accuracy," Mr. Thomas Altshuler, vice-president of Teledyne Co. builder of the "black boxes" audio pinger beacon(s) and audio pinger detection locating devices, verified that both devices are tuned to approximately 37.5 KHZ. Mr. David Stupples, an engineer with City University of London, England, voices his approval, by speaking on the sophistication of the design of Phoenix International's US built "TPL" (towed underwater by Australia's *Ocean Shield* search ship), being more reliable and far superior (compared to the Chinese hand-held underwater microphone), because of its ability to operate one mile above the 4,500-meter depth of the Indian Ocean sea floor, where the audio pingings are emitted from (and it also has a maximum operating depth of twenty thousand feet).

Mr. David Gallo of "Woods' Hole Oceanographic Institute" and a scientist having previous experience, in deep-ocean, sea-floor crashed aircraft component(s) recovery/retrieval, is now optimistic about locating the two "black boxes," due to all three audio pingings having a frequency of 37.5 KHZ, at one-second intervals, all from flight 370.

Seeking further verification of the "audio pingings," confirmed earlier today by chief air marshall (Ret.) Angus Houston, Wolf Blitzer is now interviewing Captain Mark Weiss, Boeing- 777 pilot, Peter Goelz, former NTSB (US National Transportation Safety Board) managing director, and Tom Fuentes, former assistant director of the FBI. All three experts agree that the three "audio pinging" incidences (three beacons emitting at 37.5 KHZ, and at one per second time intervals), are consistent with black box beacon pinger emissions.

Tom Forman is further examining the radar gap from the country of Indonesia, needed to trace the flight path of missing MA flight no. MH-370. Using his computerized virtual imaging monitor, Tom explains, virtually and visually, how the vanished B-777, simply turned left (port), and flew west over and across Southern Thailand, but north of Indonesia's radar range, and then turned south (left/port again), still beyond and outside of Indonesia's western radar range, over the Indian Ocean, eventually flying west of the Australian continent, on a southerly heading. (See page 29.)

According to the Inmarsat Satellite Company's scientific analysis of the six and one half "handshake" communications with flight no. MH-370, the B-777 ditched onto/into the Indian Ocean, possible out of fuel. No one knows if the 239 passengers and crew were conscious or possibly unconscious?

Later, Captain Jim Tilmon, and Mr. Bill Nye, former Boeing Aircraft Manufacturing Company engineer, conversing with Don Lemon, reveal they are relying on trusting science and scientific reasonings (based on engineering specialists, flight dynamics, mathematicians, and other scientific technology), to assess what in fact happened to cause the loss of flight 370, and its present location.

Complicating matters, are the effects of two cyclones (named Gillian and Ivanhoe), presently circling the area of the current search field, according to Meteorologist Chad Myers and Ms. Kyra Phillips, CNN anchorwoman. Cyclones are hurricanes, problematic, due to the disruption(s) to potential floating aircraft wreckage or debris being dispersed, by high winds, ocean-surface wave action(s), and changing ocean currents.

Finally, and adding to the controversy, on day no. 32 of missing flight no. MH-370, is a report from Angus Houston in Australia, at 11:15 PM (EDT) in the United States and simultaneously, the next day in Australia, at 11:15 AM (day no. 33), on Tuesday, April 8, 2014 (Australian Time Zone).

PART 25

The search report of Angus Houston (chief air marshall, ret.), is being broadcast on day no. 33, Tuesday, April 8, 2014, 11:15 AM (Perth, Australia Time Zone). Angus is stating there has been an inability to relocate the pingings detected by *Ocean Shield* over the past weekend (Saturday, April 5 and Sunday, April 6, 2014), as they attempted a different angle of attack yesterday (Monday, April 7, 2014), in order to establish a second line of reference, necessary to form a triangulation to pinpoint the precise location of the black box.

Ms. Erin Burnett is allowing her expert guest, a manufacturer of "black box beacon pingers," to demonstrate the result(s) of plunging a "pinging device," into a container of water. The pinger "pings" immediately, and at the rate of one ping per second of time, being audiologically emitted (and transmitted), to the "TPL" receiver.

Rob McCallum, underwater search specialist, says sound waves are effected by various factors, including temperature swings, pressures, and underwater ocean currents. Sometimes these factors can, and do, move Sound waves ninety degrees, thereby causing greater difficulties pin-pointing the point of origination of the "audio pinging(s)" emitted from "black box beacons." Underwater sound waves behave differently than atmospheric sound waves behavior.

Ms. Jean Casarez, CNN correspondent, interviewed by Carol Costello, speaks of the challenges involved when searching 4,500 meters below the surface of the Indian Ocean. The topography of the ocean floor in this area, where flight 370 may have ditched, has mountain ranges, valleys, and some smooth plateau-like regions. Therefore, the search may slow and lengthen.

Adjunctly, the search field has now been reduced in size, from an area the size of Texas, to a smaller search zone, the size of Houston, Texas. This can benefit the *Ocean Shield*, as it continues its mission towing the "TPL" over the suspect search area, while making additional passes, in an effort to detect further pinging, before the "black box beacon's" batteries dwindle in electrical power, and then go silent.

However, Thomas Altshuler, VP of Teledyne Co., is hopeful that battery lifetime may be extended, due to if proper battery storage was done. Being that today is day no. 33 since flight 370 disappeared, then the "black box beacon batteries" have been continuously working for thirty-three days, emitting audio pings at the rate of one (1) per second of time, twenty-four hours a day. These batteries have a thirty-day guaranteed service-life, upon being immersed in water, but, with proper maintenance practices, may last as long as forty days!

Angus Houston, leader and chief of all search efforts, including aerial and ocean surface ships (twelve hours after his morning Perth, Australia, news conference), is now announcing new successful progress! Angus is reporting a third "pinging" has now been detected and heard, by the "TPL" towed by *Ocean Shield*"! This third pinging event lasted five minutes and thirty-two seconds.

And afterward, a fourth "pinging" was detected and heard separately from the earlier third "pinging" event! This fourth "pinging" detection was heard for, a time duration of seven minutes.

In total, the *Ocean Shield*'s TPL has heard four separate pinging detection events, all by the US Navy's "TPL" (and towed by "*Ocean Shield*"). Plus, the Chinese first "pinging" detection, heard by a handheld microphone, three Feet below the Indian Ocean surface, and later verified by the *Ocean Shield*'s TPL, equals a grand total of five separate detections heard.

A) Saturday, April 5, 2014 = First Chinese audio pinging heard,
B) Saturday, April 5, 2014 = First *Ocean Shield* audio pinging heard,

C) Sunday, April 6, 2014 = Second *Ocean Shield* audio pinging heard,
D) Tuesday, April 8, 2014 = Third *Ocean Shield* audio pinging heard,
E) Tuesday, April 8, 2014 = Fourth *Ocean Shield* audio pinging heard.

These five pinging/audio detection events will now be mathematically triangulated, all while "*Ocean Shield*" continues changing their angle of attack, and thereby crisscross the prime search zone to better pinpoint the location of both "black boxes" and the missing Boeing-777.

As black box beacon batteries diminish in electrical power, their pinging will acoustically fade, reducing their level of audio volume, until both batteries expire, certainly from day no. 33 (today), to possibly one more week, day no. 40.

Right now, fifteen search aircraft and fourteen search ships are combing the search field for evidence of tangible Boeing-777 components/debris.

* Seventh arc derived from Inmarsat satellite data analysis follows below:

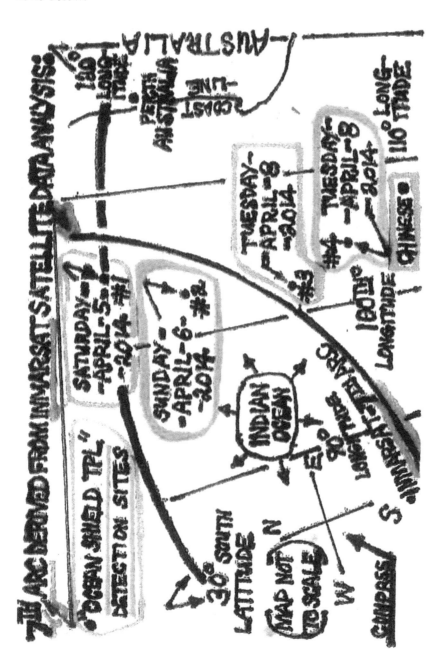

PART 26

It is Wednesday, April 9, 2014 (EDT), and day no. 34 since the missing MA flight no. MH-370 disappeared. Mr. Robert "Bob" Ballard, first person to locate the huge transatlantic passenger ship *Titanic* (that sunk to the Atlantic Sea floor after colliding with a gigantic iceberg) and speaking with Erin Burnett (Robert) says, "If the two pingings from both "black boxes" are farther apart than the length of a Boeing-777, then, the aircraft broke up (into pieces)." Robert thinks the two "black boxes" will be found and recovered. (See page 26.)

Of course, the two "black boxes" do different functions: A) FDR = Flight data recorder, B) CVR = Cockpit voice recorder.

Later, Erin also interviewed the president of the *Bluefin-21* company (a division of Phoenix International Co., and builder of the "TPL"), who agrees with Mr. Ballard's presumption. It is thought by many, the search area, scoured by the *Ocean Shield*'s TPL, and resulting in the four "pingings" detected and heard, that the sea floor of the Indian Ocean (where the four "pingings" emitted sound waves received by the "TPL"), may be covered with fine silt meters deep. Over centuries of years, fine silt compacts from ocean current(s)' movements and the tremendous pressurization encountered by over 447.38 atmospheres, at 4,500 meters of depth! (See pages 69 and 74.)

So when a submerged and sinking aircraft, or its sections of wreckage, contact this silt, if firmly and tightly compacted, then it is unlikely the wide-bodied size of a Boeing-777 would penetrate it. However, considering thirty-four days of disappearance, the possibility exists of sea floor surface disturbed silt resettling, and perhaps surrounding an aircraft as high as wing level (if intact). Conversely, smaller pieces might be buried, or partially-buried.

For good or bad, at 4,500 meters of ocean depth, it is a dark, cold, and dangerous environment. Although the darkness and fluid stillness (on the sea-floor surface) can assist the preservation of human remains, the danger factor may hamper recovery.

The world's people(s) extend their condolences to the surviving family members grieving their lost ones. Meanwhile, hundreds of dedicated good Samaritans prod on, in the search for missing MA flight no. MH-370! Including fifteen search aircraft, fourteen search ships, and countless multitudes of scientists, engineers, mathematicians, technologists, explorers, journalists, and all of their multitudinous groups of support persons, together, working to find the vanished Boeing-777!

Yet no evidence has been found for thirty-four days!

PART 27

On Thursday, April 10, 2014 (EDT), it is day no. 35.

Flight no. MH-370 has been missing for thirty-five days (five weeks)! Tom Forman is mentioning another factor concerning underwater sound wave behavior. Tom says thermally-heated areas of seawater can reflect sound waves. This can negatively affect locating "black box beacons" exact position(s) on the sea floor, thereby delaying recovery operations.

Peter Goelz, Mary Schiavo, and Richard Quest are discussing with Carol Costello a new factor that has arisen, and they offer opinion(s). The Malaysian Government MA flight no. MH-370 aircraft accident investigation team has now revealed that missing flight 370 at one time descended to a low altitude of approximately four thousand feet to five thousand feet of elevation, apparently in an effort to avoid highly trafficked aircraft lanes of flight at eighteen thousand feet and above, because with MH 370's transponder switched off, the chance of aircraft collision is increased, while collision avoidance is reduced. So four thousand feet of altitude is therefore possibly safer, but not low enough to avoid commercial radar detection.

The opinion is, the missing Boeing-777 was clearly under human control, including human control over the automatic pilot.

Coincidentally, the descent of MH-370 down to four or five thousand feet of altitude, may or may not collaborate the visual sighting of a large aircraft, thirty-five days ago, reported by a Malaysian fisherman, in his boat floating on the ocean-surface, who saw a low-flying aircraft overhead. (See page 29.)

Yesterday, an Australian P-3 aircraft deployed a "sonobuoy," which has now detected a new "ping"! This would be "ping no. six!

A "sonobuoy" floats on the ocean-surface, dangling an underwater "pinger microphone" (receiver), from one thousand feet of submerged vertical cable.

Unfortunately, "ping no. 6" is false. Upon further analysis, the "sonobuoy," placed into position Wednesday, April 9, 2014, by the Australian P-3 search aircraft, transmitted a signal, which was proven to be a false indication.

Unbelievably, Australian Prime Minister Tony Abbott may have spoken prematurely concerning the veracity of "ping no. 6." Seemingly, he spoke more as a politician (than as a scientist or oceanographer), in a search for a missing aircraft relying on ocean science and aviation sciences that define manned flight.

As mathematical triangulation calculi are being formulated, fifteen search aircraft and fourteen search ships *continue trying to find flotsam evidence.*

PART 28

On day no. 36, Friday, April 11, 2014 (EDT), Mr. John Berman, CNN anchorman, is now reporting, the search field has been reduced down to an eighteen thousand square mile search zone (about the area of New Hampshire and Vermont in the US combined), thanks to the validated four "pinging points," detected and heard by the "*Ocean Shield*'s TPL." Is this an enlargement of the previously-mentioned reduced search zone (by 1,000 percent, and being the size of Houston, Texas)? (See pages 79, 65, 63, and 62.) Now that a new prime search zone has been established, Don Lemon interviews Christine Dennison and Michael Kay, a lieutenant colonel and a British RAF pilot, concerning the ramifications involved in aircraft ocean ditchings, offering three scenarios:

1) An unpowered (engines off) nose-dive impact, which would yield tremendous damage,
2) A powered (engines running) impact, with a nose-dive, ocean-surface-entry, would yield tremendous damage, plus aircraft break-up,
3) Having an ability to deploy all flaps (enabling slower air speed), therefore allowing a possible attempt at a horizontal ocean-surface landing. If done successfully, an aircraft may have no break up, with temporary aircraft flotation.

Note 1: Scenario no. 3 was accomplished by Captain Chesley (Sully) Sullenberger III, in an emergency landing onto the surface of New York's Hudson River, with no engines running! Captain

"Sully," using a correct, horizontal, angle of attack approach, with a nose-up attitude, successfully achieved aircraft flotation, allowing 100 percent of passengers and crew to deplane onto both wings upper surfaces, to be rescued. Because all crew and passengers survived, Captain "Sully" Sullenberger's successful emergency water landing, combined with aircraft flotation, has forever been named "The Miracle On The Hudson"!

Note 2: However, far out at sea, an ocean surface, horizontal type landing is nearly impossible, in the darkness of night, because of the ten to twenty feet normal height of ocean waves' swelling, that would probably lead to an aircraft break-apart.

Mr. Rob McCallum, vice president of Williamson Associates Company, and an ocean search expert and specialist, says "searching at a depth of 4,500 meters (4.5 KM) is, "an alien world," where sunlight does not penetrate, making the AUV (autonomous underwater vehicle) search, for the two "black boxes," (the FDR and the CVR), tough but possible." Abilities engineered into the AUV include: sonar, side-scan radar, and camera photographic ability combined with high-intensity spotlights. This AUV, named *Bluefin-21*, cannot be deployed until the "TPL," towed by *Ocean Shield*, concludes its "ping" search, which hinges on "beacon pinger" battery life span.

Today, being day no. 36, means the black box beacon batteries have now exceeded their thirty-day guarantee of electrical charge after operating twenty-four hours a day for thirty-six days, leaving a maximum four-day window of chance pinging.

Additionally, David Soucie, speaking with Ashleigh Banfield, is saying the costs involved in searching for missing flight 370, may reach a point where searching, while efficient, may no longer be effective or productive.

Good news might be the fact that Malaysia Airlines Company does have a one billion dollar insurance policy with coverage for flight no. MH-370.

Possible bad news might be that in order to file a claim:

1) a loss must be proven at this time,
2) yet no Boeing-777 aircraft wreckage, debris, or flotsam has been found.

NOT A TRACE!

PART 29

Today's search area (Saturday, April 12, 2014 [EDT], day no. 37), is now the size of Massachusetts and Connecticut (two US states), combined. (See page 86.) Tony Abbott, Australian prime minister, is very confident today's fourteen search ships and ten search aircraft are on the correct track to find both "black boxes".

A three person expert panel is being convened by Fredrika Whitfield, consisting of Mary Schiavo, former assistant director of the US FAA/DOT, David Soucie, author of *Why Planes Crash*, and Mr. Alan Diehl, author of a book dealing with aircraft disasters, to discuss the value of the hard evidence, in the search for missing flight no. MH-370:

1) The British Inmarsat Satellite six and one half "handshake" communication(s), mathematical and scientific factual data/evidence, that established a southerly heading, all the way until the very last "half handshake" before ocean ditching occurred, and aircraft impact onto/into the Indian Ocean.

2) The four "pings" detected and heard by the *Ocean Shield*'s TPL, two "pings" heard one week ago, on Saturday, April 5, and Sunday, April 6, 2014 (EDT), plus two more "pings," detected and heard, five days ago, on Tuesday April 8, 2014 (EDT).

3) The "TPL," towed by Australia' *Ocean Shield* search ship will reach a day when no pingings are any longer detected or heard, after the "black box" beacon's batteries have expired.

4)   Once no more pingings are detected or heard, then the AUV (autonomous underwater vehicle) will be deployed, to embark on its underwater deep-ocean search. The "AUV" on board *Ocean Shield* is named *Bluefin-21*, and it is very-well equipped to map the Indian Ocean sea floor. Note: The AUV search could possibly take five days to five months.

Arriving now are Rob McCallum, underwater expedition leader and search specialist, and Mr. Van Gurley, of Metron Scientific Solutions, to theorize on the search schedule ahead to find flight 370. Both are unanimous that the missing Boeing-777 is 4,500 meters deep, on the sea floor of the Indian Ocean. And both agree that no more pinging has been detected or heard by the *Ocean Shield's* TPL for four days. Rob and Van say: It is now time to deploy the AUV *Bluefin-21*, from the *Ocean Shield*, to locate both "black boxes" and/ or the B-777, from the four and one-half kilometer depths of the Indian Ocean.

How deep is four and one half kilometers? How deep is 4,500 meters? Ed Lavandera provides such answers! Ed says 4,500 meters equals 14,800 feet. The *Titanic* by comparison, was found on the sea floor of the North Atlantic Ocean at a depth of 12,500 feet. Also, Ed says "Mt. Ranier" is less high than "the black box pinging is deep." Precisely, 4,500 meters equals 14,763-plus feet.

Mr. Paul Ginzberg, audio expert, is presenting a scientific demonstration of how "audio enhancement filtration" allows audio specialists to detect and hear "pinging," while the "pinging" is being masked by "white noise" that exists within our Earth's oceans. Some "white noise" is produced by humans, such as ships and/or sonar-in-usage, but the remainder of "white noise" is produced by nature, such as sea-life, oceanic conditions, and even meteorological input, made by rainfall. Paul also speaks of how sound waves can and are bent, refracted, and reflected by water thermal layers, ocean salinity, and ocean currents, all without "white noise" added.

All the above-listed factors may/can influence the detection of "black box" pinging, thereby making scientifically factual data more difficult to mathematically triangulate the precise site of the two "black boxes" and their aircraft wreckage.

The finding of missing MA flight no. MH-370 is said to be: "The most difficult search in history" (CNN). Today (day no. 37), the United States has now already spent 7.1 million dollars searching for flight 370. China, Australia, Great Britain, New Zealand, Japan, and France have all spent significant millions of dollars as well.

Interestingly, Malaysia is reported to have spent the least. Nationalized Malaysia Airlines have received $250,000,000 to $300,000,000 in payments, while possessing an additional one billion dollars in insurance coverage(s) for liabilities to passengers. Yet Malaysia Airlines has only paid out five thousand dollars per passenger to surviving family members.

Mr. Bob Francis, former vice chairman, NTSB, speaking with Fredrika Whitfield, is stating that some countries with the necessary financial assets and advanced technological search equipment may need years to locate the vanished Boeing-777, MA flight no. MH-370.

PART 30

It is now Sunday, April 13, 2014 (EDT), and day no. 38, as Will Ripley, reporting to Ms. Candy Crowley, is stating that the total monthly cost, by all countries actively participating in the Indian Ocean search for missing flight no. MH-370 is now approximately twenty-one million dollars.

The two "black boxes" on board missing flight 370, should now be transitioning from beacon pinger emission with charged batteries to unfortunately beacon pinger battery electrical power expiration, after thirty-eight days of continual usage. (Forty days maximum output on a thirty-day guarantee.)

Once Chief Air Marshall Angus Houston is certain the "beacon pinger" battery(ies) have completely expired, then the "AUV" underwater search for both "black boxes," and/or B-777-aircraft wreckage, can begin. The "AUV" search can take two weeks to as long as two years. (See page 90.)

Then, upon locating the Boeing-777 aircraft and/or its "black box(es)," the next stage can commence: recovery utilizing "ROVs." "ROVs" are remotely operated vehicle(s), capable of grasping objects with manipulators.

PART 31

Monday becomes day no. 39, April 14, 2014 (EDT). Angus Houston is holding a news conference, from Australia, to announce four points, as follow:

1) An oil slick has now been found, within the pinging perimeter of the prime search zone. A sample has been taken for study and analysis (to see if it matches any oil(s) used on Boeing-777s).

2) Tomorrow (day no. 40), the "TPL" should be concluding its "pinging search," while still being towed by the Australian *Ocean Shield* search ship. (The thirty-day battery guarantee, after forty days of constant usage, would be completely drained of electrical power.)

3) Once finished, the "TPL" will switch searching duties with the "AUV" on board *Ocean Shield*. THE AUV named *Bluefin-21* will then begin its daunting underwater search.

4) The AUV *Bluefin-21*'s assignment will be to search a 15.4 square mile section of the prime pinging zone, by mapping the sea-floor.

David Soucie, conversing with Ms. Michaela Peireira, CNN anchorwoman, is confirming that the TPL (towed pinger locator), will now be discontinued, after not detecting or hearing additional pinging for the last six days.

David is also verifying that the AUV *Bluefin-21* has indeed been deployed by *Ocean Shield* on Monday, April 14, 2014 (EDT), day no. 39. The *Bluefin-21* will begin working with its sonar searching abilities. Tom Forman, explaining the dynamics involved in the AUV search for missing flight no. MH-370, reports that *Bluefin-21*, actually, will be a sea floor mapping mission within the pinging zone, near the floor of the Indian Ocean.

* The schedule of the AUV sea floor mapping mission for *Bluefin-21* is as follows:

A) Two hours needed for the AUV *Bluefin-21* to descend, 90 percent of the distance, to the sea floor,

B) Sixteen hours needed for *Bluefin-21*'s SONAR to scour and map, the three-mile by five miles (15.4 sq. mi.) sea floor area of the Indian Ocean, within the pinging zone detected by the "TPL" (see page 93),

C) Two hours needed for *Bluefin-21* to ascend upward, to return to the *Ocean Shield* search ship,

D) Four hours needed to download the computerized sonar imagery of the sea-floor mapped,

E) Twenty-four hours, total AUV cycle time, plus, more time necessary to tune up the "AUV,"

F) "X" hours needed to recharge/change out the AUV *Bluefin-21*'s batteries (coinciding with "AUV" tune-up time).

More dynamics of the "AUV" search as follows:

1) The pinging zone, previously detected by the "TPL" (towed pinger locator), towed by the Australian search ship *Ocean Shield*, is emanating from a sea-floor depth of four and one-half kilometers = 4,500 meters = 14,764 feet;

2) At this depth, it is dark (pitch-black), with no sea-life, and the water temperature is near freezing cold,

3) Fortunately, this deep-water environment is very still, with virtually no current(s), benefiting *Bluefin-21*'s" sea-floor mapping mission,

4) Unfortunately, the ocean surface of the Indian Ocean, where the *Ocean Shield* will now be operating as a "control mother ship" for the AUV *Bluefin-21*, has storms, winds, currents, and sea-swells (large waves).

Ms. Pamela Brown, CNN correspondent, is now reporting an interesting fact, concerning the co-pilot's cellphone being turned on and possibly being used during the time span of the disappearance of Malaysia Airlines flight 370. The co-pilot's cellphone activation was detected by a cellphone tower, located in Penang, Malaysia, 250 miles distant from the point of flight 370 transponder turn off. *Why? Is this a factor? A clue?*

This is controversial, in that, this cell-tower indication occurred while flight 370, co-incidentally, descended in altitude, down to as low as four thousand to five thousand feet, in the area where the Malaysian fisherman, floating on the Indian Ocean in his boat, said he visually sighted a large, low-flying aircraft on day no. 1 of the vanished Boeing-777, when it last flew on Friday, March 7, 2014 (EST)/Saturday, March 8, 2014 (Malaysia Time Zone). (See pages 24, 29, and 84.)

Pamela, additionally, is interested in the oil-slick found, within the Indian Ocean surface of the pinging perimeter of the prime search zone. (See page 93.) So she is now interviewing Thomas Altshuler, of Teledyne Co., and Mr. David Kelly, engineer of *Bluefin-21* (AUV built by Phoenix International Company). They both spoke of how the oil slick (if from the engines of a Boeing-777), after laboratory analysis, will have specific viscosities and parameters designated by the engine manufacturer: Rolls-Royce Company. Contrarily, should the oil sample, after analysis, prove to be hydraulic oil, it will be nonflammable, SAE-10w oil approved by the B-777 manufacturer: Boeing aircraft manufacturing company (builder of the B-777, that is/was MA flight no. MH-370).

(Note: A B-777 Rolls-Royce engine contains twenty liters of lubricating motor oil.)

Also, although today is Monday, April 14, 2014 (EDT), and day no. 39 since MA flight no. MH-370 went missing, it is day no. 1 of the AUV *Bluefin-21* joining in, the Odyssey of the daunting search, for the vanished Boeing-777. As mentioned, *Bluefin-21* will map the sea floor, hoping to discern the form of an aircraft.

PART 32

So now it is day no. 40, Tuesday, April 15, 2014 (EDT), and day no. 2 of the AUV search by *Bluefin-21*. However, today the launching of *Bluefin-21* is being delayed, due to inclement weather conditions within the present search zone, where the Australian search ship *Ocean Shield* is now positioned, according to Carol Costello.

Yesterday, *Bluefin-21*'s first launching into the Indian Ocean, began by utilizing its own on-board-sonar, to search the sea-floor, to start its mapping mission. It was concluded after only seven and one-half hours, for its own safety. Apparently, *Bluefin-21* dove too deeply, beyond and below its targeted and programmed safe diving depth. The cost of the *Bluefin-21*, plus its research and development (R+D) phase, exceeds many millions of dollars. And there is only one such AUV on-board the *Ocean Shield*. Exercising much caution, the *Bluefin-21*'s own on board computer ordered it to surface!

Upon surfacing, the seven and one-half hours of its data was downloaded and analyzed aboard *Ocean Shield*. *Bluefin-21*'s first day search data found zero, in its quest to locate missing flight 370.

Mr. Chris Cuomo is interviewing David Soucie, concerning the abilities of the AUV *Bluefin-21* (which was loaned by the US Navy).

David tells Chris, the *Bluefin-21* AUV has a maximum operating depth of 14,900 feet. The "TPL" (also loaned by the US Navy), towed by the Australian Navy's search ship *Ocean Shield*, has established the depth of the black box beacon's pingings, to have emanated from 4 ½ KM = 4,500 Meters = 14,764 feet

Using subtraction, the AUV *Bluefin-21* would, therefore, operate, its search, with a pressure safety buffer margin of 136 feet.

Jake Tapper is now directing the question, "Is the *Bluefin-21* the proper AUV for the flight 370 search?," to Rob McCallum and David Soucie. Both gentlemen, Rob, an expert underwater ocean expedition leader, and David, author and aviation analyst, agree the *Bluefin-21* can rapidly locate the Boeing-777 aircraft wreckage, or conversely, rapidly eliminate the site. Therefore, the search team has a very good, high probability chance of locating missing flight 370.

Because of the delay, due to inclement weather, launching the *Bluefin-21* from the *Ocean Shield* today, Don Lemon, together with Les Abend, active B-777 pilot, and Jim Tilmon, retired pilot, now announce *Bluefin-21*'s new dive schedule.

On day no. 2 of *Bluefin-21* diving to map the sea-floor: 10:00 AM launch from *Ocean Shield* on Tuesday, April 15, 2014 (EDT) to 10:00 AM return, to *Ocean Shield*, on Wednesday, April 16, 2014 (EDT). A full twenty-four-hour mapping mission.

* Monday, day no. 1 = seven and one-half hours mapping the sea floor,

- Tuesday, day no. 2 = twenty-four hours mapping the sea floor,
- Monday + Tuesday = a total of thirty-one and one-half hours mapping the sea floor.
- This would equal (=) an average fifteen and three-quarter hours for the two days of mapping the sea floor, which is close to the planned and scheduled sixteen-hour, daily sea floor mapping search mission. (See page 94.)

An alternative AUV searching method solution follows:

If the sea floor of the Indian Ocean is too deep for the *Bluefin-21* to operate safely (where the B-777 is said to have come to rest), then a towed AUV, having an operating depth of twenty thousand feet below the ocean surface, could be working the search zone. A towed AUV can be advantageous, in that, it never has to surface daily for battery maintenance and computerized reprogramming (necessary to send the *Bluefin-21* AUV to a particular zone in a particular fashion). Additionally, its tow cable does three functions:

1) Continuously towing the AUV twenty-four hours/seven days weekly,
2) Delivering higher electrical cable voltages, thereby powering enhanced, larger sonar, that can map larger search areas,
3) And it transmits continuous live streaming imagery (perhaps photographic/video/digital), and other information.

Notwithstanding today's state-of-the-art, twenty-first century, highly-technologically advanced stratagem, being employed in the ongoing search for missing MA flight no. MH-370, Anderson Cooper is, comparatively, featuring an earlier technology, now-retired, submersible. It is the "Harbor Branch," two man submarine, having a pressure-resistant spherical cockpit.

It has mechanically-operated "pincers" on "arms," plus, a vacuum tube to collect small items. It holds sufficient oxygen, food, and potable water for a five-day underwater mission, with the ability to descend, approximately three thousand meters. (Note: 3,000 meters equals 9,842 ½ feet equaling 1,500 meters shy of *Bluefin-21*'s descent abilities.)

Because of the mysterious and disastrous plight of missing flight no. MH-370, Carol Costello raises the topic of current, and future aircraft in-flight safety methodologies. Consulting with Mary Schiavo, David Soucie, and Rob McCallum, Mary speaks about a new safety measure named "ADS-B". "ADS-B" is an air transportation control system, featuring an aircraft, equipped with a GPS (global positioning system) tracking system. (Note: By definition, GPS refers to a global, twenty-four Earth geo-synchronous, orbiting and interconnected satellite system). The twenty-four geo-synchronous satellites orbit at an altitude of 12,500 miles above the Earth, placed four-per-orbit, evenly spaced into six orbits, at varying latitudes of the Earth, and working in harmony with the aircraft on-board GPS (global positioning system) unit, mounted within the aircraft, flying at its proper elevation of flight. "ADS-B" is a portion of the long-awaited implementation of "next generation" of aircraft operation and safety, (nicknamed "next-gen").

"Next Generation" (next-gen) may consist of the following:

1) The above-described "ADS-B" (aircraft with GPS) (see page 99)
2) In-cockpit cameras capable of live-streaming imagery to Earth-orbiting satellites, and memorizing action(s) in the cockpit (see page 72)
3) Replacing twentieth century "black boxes" with twenty-first century direct air to ground, or air to satellite live-streaming data feed for both "FDR" and "CVR," (flight data recorder and cockpit voice recorder). (See pages 57, 75, and 99.)

Such Revelations make it incumbent to imagine/visualize:

A) Using "ADS-B" = knowing the precise aircraft location,
B) In cockpit cameras = knowing by video, any cockpit subterfuge,
C) Live streaming = knowing all FDR data, and CVR data, of all cockpit events, now,
D) * The "icing on the cake" = no more black box searchings!

Meanwhile, analysis of the two-liter oil sample, lifted from the oil slick discovered and whisked to the laboratory continues, in hope(s) of identically matching The "mil specs" (military specifications), required by Boeing Co., and Rolls-Royce Co. as fourteen search aircraft, and eleven search ships, continue trying to visually spot B-777 flotsam by moving westward.

PART 33

As our sun rises, gradually dawning over and above all the countries of our Earth, while it becomes day no. 41, of the mysterious disappearance of flight no. MH-370, on Wednesday, April 16, 2014 (EDT); also, it is day no. 3, in the odyssey of *Bluefin-21* mapping the sea floor in the prime search zone of the Indian Ocean. The odyssey of *Bluefin-21*, mapping the sea floor, was temporarily overwhelmed, briefly, on its first day, April 14, 2014 (EDT), when it surfaced prematurely after seven and one-half hours of sonar usage, deep underwater. Today, Peter Goelz is explaining to Wolf Blitzer that *Bluefin-21* suffered a technical glitch.

Then, Brian Todd verified to Wolf that *Bluefin-21*'s mechanics discovered a low oil level inside one of the electronics compartments and added oil to specifications. Also, they reprogrammed its on-board computer to dive to its correct depth. On *Bluefin-21*'s second day dive, it successfully mapped the sea-floor with its on-board sonar for twenty hours, thereby allowing for today's (day no. 3) planned, twenty-hour sonar-mapping mission. Also disclosed, AUV manufacturer, Phoenix international is now stating, their *Bluefin-21* may be able to be programmed, to dive a little deeper.

Yet they are mindful of the 14,900-foot depth limit, adhered to for implosion prevention, protecting their multimillion dollar *Bluefin-21*, and not compromising the all-important sea-floor mapping mission, necessary to locate the missing B-777.

The consistency of the sea-floor, within the prime search zone, is dark with a granular silt. Mr. Murtugudde, ocean scientist, is saying to Ms. Christine Romans, CNN correspondent, that a plateau-like, silty sea-floor is a very much preferred searching environment, com-

101

pared to exploring underwater mountains and canyons. However, perhaps after ocean-surface contact, as the descending Boeing-777 aircraft wreckage, of missing Malaysia Airlines flight no. MH-370, reaches the sea-floor, the great weight encountered at 450 atmospheres of pressure will/may help push its debris/wreckage into the Granular Silt.

Thomas Altshuler, of Teledyne Remote Communications Division, and Peter Goelz, Fmr. managing director of the US NTSB, both tell Carol Costello that a shiny, metallic, and brightly painted aircraft, with rectangular components, is easily viewed, contrasted against a dark, silty background.

Regarding the two-liter oil sample, taken from the search area oil slick, and presently undergoing analysis, Mr. Murtugudde now mentions the subject of decomposition. Thermal effect combined with the intense pressurization of 450 atmospheres at 14,800 feet of water depth, may decompose the sample oil's consistency.

As mentioned, today is day no. 41, and day no. 3 of *Bluefin-21*'s daunting sea floor mapping mission. But what happens if the vanished flight no. MH-370 is discovered in significantly deeper ocean waters? Well, there are four deeper-diving contingency alternatives, as follow:

1) The *Orion* Towed AUV (Maximum diving depth = twenty thousand feet). (See pages 98 and 99).
2) The *Remus-6000* AUV (Maximum diving depth = twenty thousand feet).
3) The Chinese *Sea-Dragon* AUV (Maximum diving depth = 4.4 miles).
4) The Russians' two *Soyuz* AUVS (maximum diving depth = uncertain).

Many feel *Bluefin-21* can handle its assignment. Ms. Sylvia Earle, of the National Geographic Society, and Mary Schiavo, Fmr. asst. director of the US FAA/DOT, both understand the 14,900 feet diving depth limitations of *Bluefin-21*. But because the *Ocean*

Shield's TPL indicated a pinging depth of four and one-half kilometers = 14,764 feet, they both agree the depth of the four pingings, detected on April 5, 6, and 8, 2014 (EDT), are above *Bluefin-21*'s depth limitations (by a 136-foot buffer margin of safety), and therefore, searchable and mappable. (See pages 98 and 74.)

Could the sea floor be mapped more rapidly
by using a squadron of several AUVs?

Tom Forman is examining the geographical logistics, and mathematical ramifications involved in the coordinating of a squadron of AUVs, similar to *Bluefin-21*, being deployed to map the sea floor of the Indian Ocean.

For example, the costs of deploying and operating a half-dozen AUVs (similar to *Bluefin-21*), would include the multiplying by a factor of six, the cost(s) of a single *Bluefin-21* AUV, and involve approximately ten personnel per AUV. Additionally, the launching of three to six more mother control search-ships, plus, possibly as many as sixty more engineers, mechanics, and technologists, who are familiar with underwater oceanography, and advanced control computerization techniques and methodologies.

Brooke Baldwin is now asking aviation analysts Mr. Richard Gillespie, and Mr. David Wise (a science writer): "Did Malaysia Airlines flight no. MH-370 contain the correct "black boxes" according to the serial numbers listed on the "black boxes" themselves?" They both answered, the serial numbers would be itemized within the maintenance records, and/or the log books for that particular aircraft. However, the Malaysians are uncooperative in this regard.

Tom Fuentes, Fmr. Asst. Director of the US FBI, is now addressing the minimal money (five thousand dollars), provided to the surviving family members (next of kin), by Malaysia Airlines. Tom is also referencing the fact that the missing (or lost) passengers on board missing flight no. MH-370, may have been the main breadwinners, that those same surviving next-of-kin family members relied on for financial support. (See page 91.)

Brooke, now, is examining, by invitation, Mr. Arthur Rosenberg, *Esquire*, concerning the legalities involved in the compensation to next-of-kin, family surviving members. Mr. Rosenberg states for a wrongful death lawsuit to be heard in a United States courtroom, Boeing Aircraft Manufacturing Company would have to have some guilt, in the design, or the manufacture of their Boeing-777-200 series (model), aircraft, proving Boeing's negligence, having caused that Malaysia Airlines flight no. MH-370 to crash, and go missing on March 8, 2014 (day no. 1, Malaysia Time Zone). Should flight no. MH-370 aircraft wreckage be found in the depths of the Indian Ocean, then either negligence by Boeing Co., might be proven, or not proven.

If not proven, then the aircraft's owner, Malaysia Airlines, would be found to be liable, to the surviving family(ies)' next of kin, in the payment of monetary compensation for wrongful death. Wrongful death would then have to be proven in Malaysia, under Malaysian Law, in a Malaysian court of law having the correct jurisdiction. (See page 91.)

At this six-week point of the total disappearance of MA flight no. MH-370, the costs to all the countries involved, and those actively participating in the search are now approaching, and/or exceeding, a monthly total expense of $21,000,000. (See page 92.)

ISTANBUL - May 28: A Malaysia Airlines Boeing 777 takes off on May 28, 2014 in Istanbul. This aircraft is the sister airplane of the plane missing in the Indian Ocean with the registration 9M-MRO.

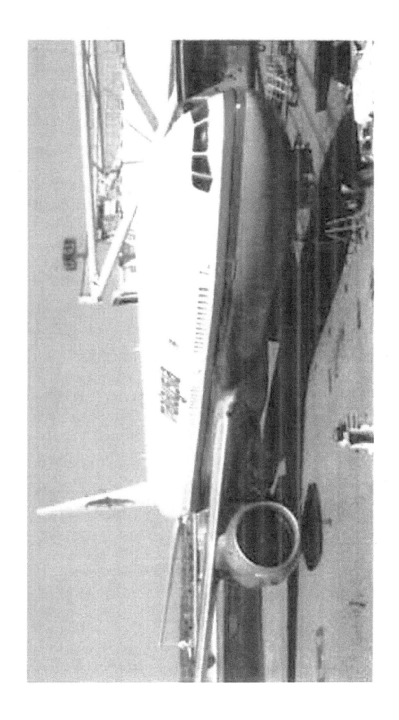

PART 34

Another day, Thursday, April 17, 2014 (EDT). It is day no. 42, and six weeks of flight no. MH-370 missing after departing Kuala Lumpur International Airport. It is also day 4, of *Bluefin-21* mapping the sea floor, below the Indian Ocean surface. Jake Tapper reports, If AUV *Bluefin-21* should be unsuccessful mapping the triangulated search zone, derived from the mathematical calculations of Inmarsat Satellite Co. and the four pingings detected by the "TPL" towed by *Ocean Shield*, then, an extended six-month search could cost $250,000,000.

But Pamela Brown is now telling Wolf Blitzer good news: *Bluefin-21* has had a very successful day 4, mapping the sea floor twelve hours earlier than EST/EDT, in the Indian Ocean/Australian border, time zone area. Pamela is stating next, that *Bluefin-21*, during its four days submerged, diving deep, has mapped forty-six square miles of Indian Ocean sea floor, within the triangulated prime search zone.

Lastly, Pamela reassures the World's population, that after completing its data download and battery recharge, *Bluefin-21* will again dive into its day 5 exploration, some 3,200 to 4,600 meters deep, into the darkness of the abyss, called the Indian Ocean.

Three hours earlier, the results of the two liter oil sample, taken from the surprise discovery of the oil slick amid the search area, were announced, following analysis completion. In the beginning, the skimmed oil sample was hurriedly, both, shipped and helicoptered to a laboratory located in Perth, Australia. The test results announced were negative. After analysis, the hydrocarbons found in the two liter oil-slick sample did not match the formulations, recommended by

Rolls Royce Co., for usage in their jet- engine lubrication(s). Nor was there a hydrocarbon match, for the hydraulic oil(s), approved by Boeing Co. for usage in their Model-777 Series aircraft.

Mr. David Mattingly, speaking with Anderson Cooper, is now inside a three-man submersible, capable of manipulation(s). In the command module of this particular submersible, David is accompanied by one of the originators of submersible manipulation, Mr. Phil Nuyjen. Phil is demonstrating the very agile and tedious process, of mechanical manipulation, necessary to grasp and place a black box into a collection receptacle, and/or basket.

And so ends day no. 42. *But without MH-370's 239 passengers and crew!*

PART 35

Today is day no. 43 in the disappearance of Malaysia Airlines missing flight no. MH-370, and day 5 of *Bluefin-21* mapping the sea floor, within the prime search zone, mathematically triangulated. Today, Friday, April 18, 2014 (EDT), a summary of the five search methods, that have been utilized to locate and recover the wide-bodied B-777, and/or its two "black boxes" follow:

1) Not helpful = satellite visual scanning of our Earth and Indian Ocean area,

2) Helpful = the ocean-surface search for aircraft wreckage, performed daily for six weeks, by fourteen search aircraft and twelve search ships,

3) Very helpful = Inmarsat Satellite Company's electronic six and one half "handshakes," between Inmarsat's geosynchronous satellite(s) and MA flight no. MH-370, that allowed Inmarsat scientists to chart a very precise flight path, indicating a southerly heading to the Indian Ocean,

4) Very helpful = the Australian search ship *Ocean Shield*, that towed the US Navy's "TPL," which detected the four black box signature pingings, enabling the search team's scientists to mathematically triangulate a prime search zone, culminating in the *Bluefin-21* AUV sea floor mapping mission,

5) Very helpful = the *Bluefin-21* AUV'S Indian Ocean Sea floor mapping mission.

Also, Angus Houston is rumored to now call off, at least, the very expensive aerial search, (aircraft portion), for B-777 floating wreckage, possibly tomorrow.

Two hours later (today), Brooke Baldwin is now interviewing Capt. Van Gurley, US Navy, Ret., and Chad Myers, CNN meteorologist, all in discussion, concerning the expansion of the search area. The discussion entails eventually extending the seventeen mile by fifteen-mile prime search zone, to a search field of 320 miles by 500 miles. (See pages 86, 79, 65, and 62.)

Now Brooke is speaking with Richard Quest. They are examining the four ELTs (emergency locator transmitters), on board flight 370. As to the subject of four ELTs, strangely and oddly, the four ELTs on board flight 370, never sounded, nor transmitted data.

Yet an ELT is designed to trigger transmissions upon either: impact or impact with water (as an ocean, for example).

Again, the profundity of why MA flight no. MH-370 disappeared, not only deepens, it appears to be broadening in the scope of its narrative!

Broadening, in that, cockpit control must have limitations over the miles and miles of the electrical wiring and circuitry, engineered into the very advanced Boeing-777, for passenger and flight crew safety in flight:

A)   Each pilot can turn off the transponder, in case of cockpit-fire or other electrical emergency(ies),

B)   But the ACAR/ACART system, wired to both engines, should always be working, together with existing Earth-orbiting satellites,

C)   And emergency locator transmitters (ELTs), always need to be working, should the aircraft experience sudden ditching,

D)   Of course, "black boxes" furnish answers, during unexpected death(s) arising from a crash scenario. (Until next-generation "ADS-B" satellite tracking, with GPS, can be implemented.) (See page 100.)

The four ELTS on-board Boeing-777s are inconspicuously mounted, inside the aircraft's nose, its tail assembly, and mid-fuselage, and are not readily or easily accessible. They are accessed by mechanics having location knowledge and proper authorization(s).

PART 36

So now it becomes day no. 44, in the banishment of flight no. MH-370 from all sight and sound. *Bluefin-21* dove twice today, Saturday, April 19, 2014 (EDT), and day 6 of its sea floor mapping mission. Its first dive today ended abruptly, when a technical glitch arose, causing it to resurface, for the requisite adjustment, and/or, repair. After engineering and the mechanics' work were completed, *Bluefin-21* was relaunched on dive 7, during day no. 6 of mapping.

Fredrika Whitfield is consulting with a three-person expert panel:

A) Mr. Fabien Cousteau, oceanographer, says a reexamination of all known facts, including a recalculation of Inmarsat Satellite "handshake(s)" data, must be done,

B) Jeff Wise, author, states: if *Bluefin-21* does not locate missing flight no. MH-370, within one more week (totaling two weeks mapping), then a regrouping of search strategy must be implemented,

C) Tom Fuentes, FBI-retired assistant director, reports skepticism, of all the radar information, concerning missing flight no. MH-370.

PART 37

Today, Sunday, April 20, 2014 (EDT), is also day no. 45 in the continuing saga of MA flight no. MH-370's disappearance. *Bluefin-21* is executing dive no. 8, on its seventh day of exploring the Indian Ocean, within the primary search zone, triangulated for sea floor mapping.

However, the secondary Indian Ocean floating wreckage search area has moved westward. Today's ocean-surface search, has eleven search aircraft and ten search ships scouring the seas for any evidence of the vanished Boeing-777, and/or its 239 missing occupants. Moving the ocean surface search to the west gives plenty of open space to *Ocean Shield*, and its *Bluefin-21* mapping mission.

Sadly at the conclusion of day no. 45, not a single piece of tangible evidence of a downed B-777 has yet to be located! *Not a trace!* The condition of the surviving families of the missing 239 passengers and crew must be unbearable! *The globe asks, how? Why?*

PART 38

As of today, Monday, April 21, 2014 (EDT), and day no. 46, *Bluefin-21* has successfully mapped two-thirds of the prime pinging search zone, of the sea floor at the bottom of the Indian Ocean! Today, Monday, *Bluefin-21* is on its ninth dive, on its day 8, of its mapping assignment. That particular good news is tempered, because there is still no trace of tangible Boeing-777 wreckage, or physical evidence of missing flight 370.

According to Mr. Miguel Marquez, today's ninth dive by *Bluefin-21* encompassed a 115–square mile area, as triangulated from data gathered by *Ocean Shield's* TPL mission, that detected four pings.

Peter Goelz states, that, if the final one-third of the prime search zone (as mathematically triangulated from, the four "pingings," detected and heard, by *Ocean Shield's* TPL mission), proves to shed no evidence of the missing Boeing-777, then a search reassessment needs to be studied and implemented, to Wolf Blitzer.

And Tom Fuentes adds, Malaysia Airlines should begin the process of real compensation to the distraught next of kin (of the surviving family members), of the missing 239 people on board vanished flight no. MH-370.

Additionally, Mary Schiavo spoke on the differing altitudes flown by missing flight no. MH-370, during its final flight of disappearance, ranging from thirty-nine thousand feet, to as low as four to five thousand feet, as unusually low for a Boeing-777 to Erin Burnett. (See pages 95, 84, and 33.)

Richard Quest responds, with the possibility, that missing flight 370 might have flown northward, along the Inmarsat Satellite's

Northerly Arc. (Note: Inmarsat's Satellite-established "northern arc" and its "southern arc" are (both together), globally, longitudinally, contiguous.)

Everyone knows weather conditions change. Earlier today, M, April 21, 2014 (EDT), Ms. Erin McLaughlin, reporting from Perth, Australia, spoke about a newly-emerging factor, in the search for MA MH-370. Namely, the proximity of cyclone "Jack," adjacent to *Ocean Shield*, in the Indian Ocean.

PART 39

Today, day no. 47, in the continuing story of a vanished wide-bodied, modern Boeing-777, containing its 239 missing human occupants, there is now "good news" and "bad news."

The "bad news" is approaching cyclone "Jack" will interfere today with the deployment of both the aerial (aircraft) search, as well as the ocean-surface search-ship(s), daily surveillance mission(s), for floating Boeing-777 wreckage.

The "good news" is *Bluefin-21* will deploy on its tenth dive, of its mission day 9 effort, mapping the Indian Ocean sea floor for missing flight 370, unhindered by cyclone "Jack." As noted, it is in a different environment, submerged, near the Indian Ocean's sea floor, where submersibles, such as *Bluefin-21*, execute their heroic searching and mapping assignments(s), where the deep waters are dangerous, yet still, even while a cyclone causes surface damage and/ or destruction.

Today is Tuesday, April 22, 2014 (EDT). Twenty-eight or twenty-nine countries are participating in the search for missing flight 370, and they are sharing and splitting the high costs incurred, in a cooperative manner.

Surviving family members of the 239 missing occupants of flight 370, now are of the opinion and belief, that the Boeing-777 was hi-jacked! This would explain the absence of passengers, crew, and the Boeing-777!

PART 40

Yesterday, *Bluefin-21* continued its dive 10, in an effort to complete its examination of 80 percent of the prime search zone. Today, day no. 48, Ms. Rosemary Church, CNN anchorwoman, is now reporting that the AUV *Bluefin-21* has now surfaced, and its computers are now downloading *data* garnered, from its dive 10. Battery change out/recharging must be done (plus, any mechanical and/or digital tuning up), then dive 11 will begin to study and map the remaining 20 percent of the prime search zone, which was established by the four pingings heard by the US Navy's "TPL" mission (towed by Australia's *Ocean Shield* search ship) and guided by the analysis of Inmarsat Satellite Co.s' six and one-half "handshake(s)" communications with MA flight 370.

Day no. 48 is Wednesday, April 23, 2014 (EDT), and Ashleigh Banfield is reporting: "Breaking news: Object of interest found." Lt. Col. Michael Kay, Fmr. Royal Air Force (RAF) pilot, says, "The object found may not be of aircraft-styled construct." The object is said to be made of aluminum and having rivets plus seemingly fiberglass insulating material. However, aircraft insulation has a particular polymer identifying signature. This object will face laboratory analysis, when it arrives in Perth, Australia. Chad Myers adds the object of interest found, was gathered 1,200 miles southeast of the prime search zone. Chad further points out the object found, may actually be a composite material (now utilized on modern aircraft), rather than insulation.

Regarding (A) Related Search Dynamic (S)

A) Lt. Col. Ken Christensen, aviation consultant, tells Wolf Blitzer, if the Boeing-777 is intact, then the pings, heard seventeen miles apart, are caused by oceanic conditions, such as the following:

 1) Thermally: differentiating layers of deep water(s) (see page 78), plus,
 2) Ocean: salinity amounts, meaning underwater "rivers" of saline currents. (See page 90.)

B) Additionally, Tom Fuentes, Fmr. FBI asst. director, states the possibility, Inmarsat Satellite Data may not be publicly disclosed, in that, such data may only be interpreted, analyzed, and understood, by those scientists educated in such matters.

C) Mary Schiavo, Fmr. FAA/DOT Asst. Chief, says if the object of interest (said to be rectangular in form) is severely mangled and/or twisted, and proven to be aircraft in nature (a true Boeing-777 specimen), then, Boeing Aircraft Manufacturing Company can identify and verify their aircraft-style rivets, and high-strength alloyed steel fasteners, as well as the special three part paint (used in aircraft manufacture), should all be evident.

Regarding the separate dynamic of "live streaming"
of FDR and CVR data (flight data recorder
and cockpit voice recorder data):

All agree, it will be the United States that must take the lead, of/ in, its implementation for transoceanic flight(s). Today, the US military already has the necessary technology to implement such a "live streaming" system, for transoceanic FDR and CVR data, although it must be adapted for civilian and commercial purposes.

Existing satellite companies would eagerly embrace "ADS-B," and expanding their business operations. (See pages 100, 54, and 55.)

(Inmarsat Satellite Company is currently developing
in-flight entertainment streaming.)

* Best advantage of all, with "ADS-B" live
streaming = no more "black box" searches!

Day no. 48 becomes dusk, and Miguel Marquez, speaking from
Australia, is stating, "After Aviation Industry laboratory scrutiny
and analysis: the found object of interest is not aircraft!"

Still no trace of missing MA flight no. MH-370!

PART 41

Day no. 49 is Thursday, April 24, 2014 (EDT), and the AUV *Bluefin-21* is on its twelfth dive, mapping the sea floor, during its eleventh day underwater. At this point in time, the *Bluefin-21* is said to have completed 90 percent of the sea-floor mapping of the prime search zone, mathematically triangulated from the four "pingings," detected by the US Navy's "TPL," towed by the Australian search-ship *Ocean Shield*, based on the six and one-half "handshakes" communications, between Inmarsat's geo-synchronous Earth-orbiting satellite, and with missing MA flight no. MH-370, during its final flight.

Brooke Baldwin is interviewing Jennifer Gray concerning the next level of search submersibles, which may be utilized, should the *Bluefin-21* fail to locate, either, the missing Boeing-777, or its two "black boxes" within the prime search zone, at the Indian Ocean bottom.

Three alternate submersibles are (see page 102):

A) The *Orion* is towed by a "search mother control ship." Its tow cable has three intertwined sections. Cable section no. 1 pulls the AUV, along/near the sea floor (as deeply as twenty thousand feet), cable segment no. 2 supplies electrical energy to the *Orion* AUV, and cable segment no. 3 provides "live streaming" of imagery and informative data, from the ocean deep, back-up to the "mother control search ship."

B) The *Remus-6000* AUV (similar to the *Bluefin-21*, except *Remus-6000* dives twenty thousand feet). And *Remus-6000* also, must ascend back-up to the mother control search ship, in order to download its computerized underwater data.

C) The "ROV" (remotely operated vehicle), can be advantageous, once the target is located, because the "ROV" has manipulators. Manipulators are clamping devices, used to grasp and manipulate the objective of the target, and are, controlled by an ROV-operator, on board The "mother control search ship." The manipulators are equivalent to human arms and hands.

Ninety minutes earlier, Mr. Najib Razak, prime minister of Malaysia, is being interviewed by Richard Quest. Malaysian PM Razak is unwilling to admit, to the members of the surviving families of missing flight no. MH-370, that the vanished Boeing-777 has been lost! Although, obviously, flight no. MH-370 is missing, the surviving family members believe the passengers are still alive, perhaps because of the hi-jacking belief/theory.

According to the Malaysian PM, Malaysian radar did detect an aircraft (at the time that flight no. MH-370 flew). However, although the aircraft deviated from its flight plan (after its transponder turn off), the Malaysian military did not scramble military jets to intercept the radar-located, aircraft in flight! Because *someone* determined the aircraft was civilian, and therefore, not a security threat to the country of Malaysia!

The Malaysian Government has now completed the preliminary report, pertaining to the missing Malaysia Airlines flight no. MH-370. IT is being sent to ICAO (International Civil Aviation Organization), Montreal, Canada, and the United Nations (UN), New York City, New York, United States (NYC, NY, USA).

ICAO, meeting in the Montreal Convention, Montreal, Quebec, Canada, invoked a policy (or ruling), that for insurance compensation to be paid out: "There must exist evidence of loss" (wreckage).

PART 42

On Friday, April 25, 2014 (EDT), day no. 50, after *Bluefin-21* has concluded its twelfth dive, mapping the sea floor within the prime search zone during its eleventh day underwater, Wolf Blitzer is reporting: "The AUV has not yet turned up results indicative of a sunken Boeing-777, or either of its two "black boxes"".

Bluefin-21's twelfth dive and exploration, achieved a 95 percent sea floor mapping of the prime search zone.

Today's present thirteenth dive should complete 100 percent of the sea floor mapping mission, within the prime search zone, in/near the Inmarsat Southern Arc, and during *Bluefin-21*'s twelfth day, submerged in the profound waters of the Indian Ocean.

Also, if needed, the next stage of the search for vanished flight no. MH-370 will probably feature an expansion of ocean, beyond the prime search zone.

At 2:01 PM (EDT/EST) today, calendar verification occurred, when Brooke Baldwin announced, "Today is Day No. 50 in The Mystery of Missing Flight No. MH-370."

PART 43

Now, a next day has dawned for all corners of our planet. Of course, yesterday's tomorrow becomes today, Saturday, April 26, 2014 (EDT). And today is day no. 51 in the vanishment of MA flight no. MH-370 from all sight and sound! In fifty-one days, "conspiracy theories" have arisen and abound, since mysterious circumstances have surrounded the disappearance of flight 370:

A) Flight 370 may have landed at a US military base located at Diego Garcia, Indian Ocean,

B) A hi-jacking performed by the nation of North Korea (NK), possibly,

C) The huge Boeing-777, containing 239 Earthlings, may have fallen victim to an "alien abduction" by "extra-terrestials,"

D) Flight 370 has disappeared, due to either; no. 1) the use of an "invisibility cloak," and/or, no. 2) a "time-travel intervention."

Of course, the above-listed four (4) "theories" are (probably), all incredible, illogical, incompetent, and obscure, outrageous, outlandish rumors (See Prologue).

Earlier today, Fredrika Whitfield convened and consulted with a three-person expert panel consisting of David Soucie, Peter Goelz, and Lt. Col. Michael Kay.

The concern discussed centered on, the follow-up plan, should the *Bluefin-21* discover nothing, within the remaining 5 percent of the prime search zone:

Plan A) Move the *Bluefin-21* AUV, northward, to map the sea floor, beginning in the area of the second most likely pinging zone.

Plan B) Bring in additional submersibles, such as the *Remus-6000*. There are six *Remus-6000*s in existence. Four *Remus-6000*s are now presently under contract with the US Navy, and in constant usage. The remaining two *Remus-6000*s are located: (1) in Germany and (2) at Woods-Hole Oceanographic Institute (NE, USA).

Plan C) Bring in different "fresh minds," to operate the one or two *Remus-6000*s, as they become available, and, reexamine facts from Inmarsat data (seven "arcs" ascertained/established, from the Inmarsat scientific analysis, of the six and one-half "handshakes(s)" satellite communications, with MH-370).

Note: Regarding plan A (above), see page 81.

Regarding plan B (above), see pages 123 and 124.

Regarding plan C (above), see page 81.

PART 44

On day no. 52, today, Sunday, April 27, 2014 (EDT), United States President Barack Obama, on a four Asian nation tour, is presently visiting Kuala Lumpur, Malaysia, and its Prime Minister Najib Razak. During a press conference, President Obama did briefly mention the *horror* that missing Malaysia Airlines Flight no. MH-370 underwent, and continues to endure. In response to questioning by the Malaysian Press, Barack furnished no new answers, but did express his view, that the Malaysians are open and transparent, in doing the best capable in their investigation of the *vanished* Boeing-777.

President Obama's current Asian itinerary is

1) having departed Washington, DC;
2) President Obama visited the landslide devastation in Oso, Washington, US,
3) President Obama visited Japan and its emperor,
4) President Obama visited South Korea during its ferry capsizing accident,
5) President Obama is now visiting Kuala Lumpur, Malaysia,
6) President Obama next will visit the Philippines,
7) President Obama returns home to the USA.

PART 45

Day no. 53 is, coinciding with Carol Costello hosting and featuring Australian Prime Minister Mr. Tony Abbott, today, Monday, April 28, 2014 (EDT). Mr. Abbott is announcing, if the *Bluefin-21* (safely capable of working ocean depths of 14,900 feet), should fail to discover either "black boxes" or the submerged remains of flight 370 (a Boeing-777), then the search area would be expanded to a new search area of thirty-seven thousand square miles, with deeper depths.

- Thirty-seven thousand square miles is equivalent in size, to the state of Indiana.
- Deeper depths, as deep as twenty thousand feet.
- Ocean depths of twenty thousand feet would require the introduction of new submersibles (such as the *Remus-6000* AUV or the *Orion* AUV), to accommodate and advance the sea floor mapping mission of a broadened thirty-seven thousand square mile search field. (See pages 102, 123, and 124.)

Also, the aerial aircraft search, as well as the ocean surface ship search will now be discontinued, after greater than seven weeks of daily and dedicated surveillance, of the treacherous Indian Ocean, performed by brave humanitarian searchers.

Unfortunately, no trace of missing flight no. MH-370 was found!

PART 46

Carol Costello, reporting on day no. 54, Tuesday, April 29, 2014 (EDT), is stating an Australian company says it has found possible aircraft wreckage in the Bay of Bengal (south of the country of Bangladesh), in waters three hundred meters deep. (See map on page 134.) This Australian company, named "Geo-Resonance Co.," says it has detected a metallic indication of titanium, copper, steel, and 70 percent aluminum. Aircraft contain these metals plus other metals.

Carol, speaking with Rob McCallum and David Soucie, discovers her two guests dispute the validity of these new findings, saying the Bay of Bengal seems too far north (for flight 370 possible ditching).

"Geo-Resonance Co." (based in Adelaide, Australia), claims it used sophisticated equipment proven reliable in metal(s) detection. They first made this metallic discovery, during the second week of March 2014, about four days after the final flight, of Malaysia Airlines vanished Boeing-777, flew.

"Geo-Resonance" first notified Malaysian authorities on (or about), March 12, 2014. Then, they re-released news of their metallic findings recently, two weeks ago (April 14, 2014), publicly.

The above-described metallic discovery by Geo-Resonance Co., was disclosed this morning of Tuesday. But Tuesday afternoon, midday, possibly the most important disclosure of Geo-Resonance Co. was announced, by Wolf Blitzer, while consulting with Peter Goelz, and Tom Fuentes: Jet-A Fuel.

Jet-A Fuel is kerosene, the fuel used in the two Rolls-Royce engines, that provide thrust, and the obligatory lift, to power and fly the missing wide-bodied B-777. The two forces of Earth's nature, that prevent human flight (and must, therefore, be overcome), are no. 1) gravity and no. 2) drag.

No. 1) Gravity: Solution: Lift, provided by the airfoil design engineered into the airframe(s) of both wings, whereby while the wing bottom (underside) is basically flat the wing-top is dramatically obtusely curved, causing two different air speeds (above versus below the wing), making the necessary air pressure differentials (in conjunction with thrust), needed to cause lift.

No. 2) *Drag*: Solution: Thrust, provided by the engines exhausting rearward, thereby pushing the entire aircraft forward, overcoming the drag of Earth's thick atmosphere, which is composed of air molecules, or matter. ("Matter has mass," says Albert Einstein).

So for human flight to occur, the two solutions are:

No. 1) Lift, to overcome gravity, and no. 2) thrust, to overcome drag.

So for lift, one needs thrust. Jet-A Fuel (kerosene), powers the engines, providing thrust, and enabling lift.

After this morning's exciting announcement of Geo-Resonance Co.'s four metal discovery, came the equally (or greater), announcement of Jet-A Fuel. (Jet-A Fuel is pure kerosene basically.) Now, in the evening of the same Tuesday, day no. 54, comes more, exciting news, from Erin Burnett.

Two other metals, discovered by Geo-Resonance Co., are the exciting news; namely, chromium and molybdenum (valuable metals alloyed to the various metals, from which aircraft are constructed). Geo-Resonance Co. detected both chromium and molybdenum, by using a highly-respected and reliable and scientifically proven method of "the electromagnetic spectrum."

Chromium is added to steel, to create stainless steel. And steel is hardened and strengthened by adding molybdenum. (Steel itself is iron, alloyed with carbon and nickel).

Regarding the Jet-A Fuel discovered in the waters of the Bay of Bengal, Jet-A Fuel is the approved fuel for the engines of all jet aircraft. Conversely, boats in the Bay of Bengal having diesel engines, use diesel fuel. Diesel fuel contains an oil(y) additive, dissolved and suspended, within its kerosene, and thereby, different than Jet-A Fuel.

Therefore, Jet-A Fuel (pure kerosene), versus diesel fuel (kerosene with an oil additive), will have differing hydrocarbon signatures, enabling correct identification.

PART 47

Angus Houston, Australian chief air marshall, Ret., says, since the *Bluefin-21* AUV discovered no aircraft wreckage, after scouring 100 percent, of the prime search zone, now the findings of aircraft metals (by Geo-Resonance Co.), in the Bay of Bengal must be investigated to Wolf. The country of Bangladesh has dispatched two sonar-equipped search ships to the Bay of Bengal, to locate the discovery of aircraft-type metals and Jet-A Fuel, by Geo-Resonance Co. (See map, page 134.)

Angus Houston also is confirming the aerial (aircraft) search, for evidence of downed aircraft flotsam, has now been discontinued. However, Angus is also stating, *Bluefin-21* AUV will continue its sea floor mapping mission in the area of "TPL" located pinging no. two, and working northward toward the area of pinging no. one." (See page 81.)

Earlier, today day no. 55, and Wednesday, April 30, 2014 (EDT), Carol Costello interviewed both Miles O'Brien and Rob McCallum. Miles now says, the search team will expand, to an international level, by saying, "The finest minds in the world, in different fields of expertise, will be needed, and they all do not live in Malaysia."

Rob is skeptical of the findings of the Australian company "Geo-Resonance," because, although "The electromagnetic spectrum" method has been scientifically proven to locate metals in the Earth, their method is not known to penetrate water, while being aimed from an aircraft flying overhead, as was done.

Later, during the evening of day no. 55, under the examination of Anderson Cooper;

1) Miles O'Brien, PBS (Public Broadcasting System), chief science correspondent states: the Geo-Resonance Co. findings are not true.
2) Peter Goelz, Fmr. NTSB managing director, says, the Geo-Resonance Co. findings may be true.
3) David Soucie, author of *Why Planes Crash*, feels, surviving families members (of the 239 missing occupants of vanished flight no. MH-370), should not be misled, rather, investigate all their claims, and any other claims.

Map of the Bay of Bengal

PART 48

Today, Thursday, May 1, 2014 (EDT), day no. 56, Lt. Col. Michael Kay, RAF, retired, and Richard Quest, aviation analyst, are conversing with Ashleigh Banfield. They are discussing the release of the preliminary report, on Malaysia Airlines flight no. MH-370 (that went missing on Saturday, March 8, 2014 (Malaysia Time Zone)/ Friday, March 7, 2014 (EST).

The report states seventeen minutes elapsed, after flight no. MH-370 signed off from Malaysia's Kuala Lumpur International Airport's control tower to the scheduled sign on with Ho Chi Minh's airport's control tower. In Vietnam, Ho Chi Minh Airport's control tower realized a problem has emerged and reported flight no. MH-370, going off Vietnamese radar, without any radio communication(s).

Wolf is now stating: the report also cited a four-hour delay occurred (approximately from 1:21 AM to 5:00 AM, Malaysia Time Zone), before a search was initiated, prompted by the urgency of a missing Boeing-777 (MH-370), all due to (and because of), miscommunication(s), between authorities in Malaysia and Vietnam.

Pamela Brown reports, during the four hours that elapsed after the sign off from flight no. MH-370 to Malaysia's Kuala Lumpur Airport's Control Tower is when the missing Boeing-777's transponder, ACAR/ACART system and four ELTs (emergency locator transmitter beacons), all were deactivated!

The two time lapses (seventeen minutes; and four hours), cost much, during the disappearance of MA flight no. MH-370, and possibly are factors.

The release of the preliminary report, by Malaysian Search Authorities also contained the passenger manifest (two-Thirds of the passengers were Chinese nationals), the cargo manifest, and a transcription of the final communication(s) between MH-370 with the Kuala Lumpur Airport control tower.

The cargo manifest listed 2,500 KG of lithium-ion batteries (5,511.475 lbs.) in the cargo bay of missing MA flight no. MH-370! This type of electrical battery(ies), can be dangerous (if not properly packaged and stored for aerial transport) because they discharge/release hydrogen fluoride, a flammable hydrocarbon (fuel), according to analyses, by Miles O'Brien, David Soucie, and Richard Quest, all convened by Anderson Cooper. (See page 28.)

With respect to Mrs. Cheng Liping, thirty-eight, and Mrs. Liu Wanyi, twenty-six, two married wives, whose each husband are now among the missing passengers of flight no. MH-370, the preliminary report achieved nothing in allaying the concerns of surviving families' members, as to where is and what happened to the vanished Boeing-777, flying their 239 relatives and friends to a scheduled Beijing destination.

Unfortunately, Malaysia and China have both, now announced the closure of the family comfort centers in hotels. However, once the members of the surviving families arrive back home, the governments of both China and Malaysia will open information centers, for families, to visit and learn new facts daily, in the search for missing flight no. MH-370, and its 239 vanished passengers and crew.

For Mrs. Liu Wanyi and Mrs. Cheng Liping, it will be a bittersweet homecoming to half-empty houses, devoid of their husbands.

And possibly, coping with the potential accompanying mortification, psychologically.

PART 49

Today, Friday, May 2, 2014 (EDT), Mr. Angus Houston, Australian search team chief, is traveling to Kuala Lumpur, Malaysia, for today's noontime (Malaysia time zone), press conference, on missing MA flight no. MH-370, NOW having disappeared for fifty-seven days (including the day of its final flight on March 8, 2014 [Malaysia time zone]/March 7, 2014 [US EST]).

It is being mentioned, after all the mathematical computations of MH-370's fuel range, altitude, two engine speed factored in with drag co-efficients (weather conditions), that the missing Boeing-777, could no longer fly beyond 8:30 AM (Malaysia time zone), which is about three hours after the search was first initiated for MH-370. (Note: US EST is twelve hours later, because of our Earth's twenty-four hour west-to-east rotation.)

Phase two of the search for missing flight no. MH-370 is now projected to last a duration of eight months, utilizing "new eyes." Wolf is now interviewing a two-person expert panel, consisting of Mr. Steve Wallace, Fmr. director of US FAA accident investigation, and Tom Fuentes, Fmr. asst. director of US FBI.

Tom states, while the search team reevaluates the stage two search, seeking missing flight no. MH-370, it is important that scientists and mathematicians continue their computations to a more advanced level (in order to direct the search team with new findings and new information). Steve is stating that the reevaluation of the phase two search, will involve a meeting to be held this coming Monday, May 5, 2014 (Australia time zone). This meeting will include Malaysia, China, and Australia.

The present search (the *Bluefin-21* AUV sea floor mapping mission), may be suspended at the end of next week. The reason is to help coincide with the Australian search ship, *Ocean Shield*, returning to its Australian port for refueling and resupplying food stores, water, and maintenance. Of course, the aerial search for floating debris and wreckage by search aircraft has already been terminated last Monday, April 28, 2014, on day no. 53, of the Odyssey of missing flight no. MH-370. (See page 129).

So far, the two Bangladeshi search ships exploring the Bay of Bengal, dispatched two days ago, on Wednesday, April 30, 2014, day no. 55, have not yet found the six metals and Jet-A Fuel, detected by the Australian "Geo-Resonance Co."

The hospitality-comfort centers in hotels are closed, with the family members (of the missing 239 passengers and crew of flight no. MH-370), now homeward bound.

PART 50

Fredrika Whitfield, reporting on Saturday, May 3, 2014 (EDT), states that there is now a third Bangladeshi search ship dispatched to the Bay of Bengal. This ship will assist the two Bangladeshi sonar-equipped search ships already on scene deployed to search, explore, and hunt for any remnants of flight no. MH-370, which disappeared fifty-eight days ago.

Fredrika also verified, all hotel hospitality/comfort accommodations have closed to the surviving families, of the missing 239 passengers and crew on board vanished MA flight no. MH-370. (See page 136).

The next day, Sunday, May 4, 2014 (EDT), Fredrika Whitfield, on day no. 59, informs us, the three-nation meeting will be held in Canberra, Australia. Malaysia, China, and Australia (see page 137), will discuss the future strategy and costs, involved in the locating of missing Malaysia Airlines flight no. MH-370.

David Gallo, oceanographer with Woods-Hole Oceanographic Institute, and Mary Schiavo, fmr. asst. director of US FAA/DOT, are both still speaking optimistically today, about the finding of the disappeared Boeing-777.

PART 51

Today, on day no. 60, at Cable News Network (CNN), a three-anchor person panel—John Berman, first to report the non-arrival of flight 370 to Beijing, China, fifty nine days ago; Michaela Peireira; and Ashleigh Banfield—are reporting some important points, on Monday, May 5, 2014 (EDT), as follow below:

1) The three-nation meeting (the Malaysia, China, and Australia conference), for certain logistical reasons, will now actually begin on Wednesday, May 7, 2014, rather than today, although all representatives are in Canberra.

2) The Canberra (Australia) conference will examine the future phase two search, strategy, and costs. Regarding costs, Australia believes a one-year search extension could cost sixty-million dollars to cover an expanded search field, of a minimum twenty-three thousand square miles, to, a maximum fifty thousand to one hundred thousand square miles.

3) Additional search submersibles may be utilized during the phase two search mission. The *Remus-6000* (plus, its support and operating crews), can work at depths of twenty thousand feet, 5,100 feet deeper than the *Bluefin-21* AUV. (See pages 102, 103, 123, 124, 127, and 129.)

4) The *Bluefin-21* AUV has now completed eighteen sea floor mapping missions, covering 154 square miles of the prime search zone. The *Bluefin-21* AUV's Contract has now been extended one more month.

Meanwhile, all available, reliable data, pertaining to the disappearance of flight no. MH-370 is being reexamined and reevaluated.

Bluefin-21 AUV side scan radar illustration
(not to scale), shown below:

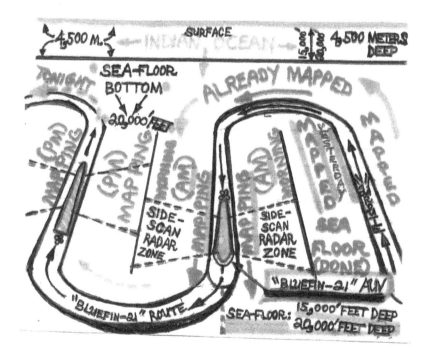

PART 52

The representatives of three nations: Malaysia, China, and Australia, are today (Tuesday, May 6, 2014, and day no. 61), now located in Canberra, Australia, preparing to convene their conference on the future of the search for the missing Malaysia Airlines flight no. MH-370. All factual, reliable data, on hand, will be reexamined, restudied, and researched:

1-(A) - DATA. Is it correct? Necessarily, search team members, and both aviation analysts and technologists, will have to return to day no. 1, Saturday, March 8, 2014 (Malaysia Time Zone)/Friday, March 7, 2014 (US EST), when the final flight of MA MH-370 flew, after the Boeing-777 departed Kuala Lumpur, for its Beijing destination, yet four hours later, it was declared to be missing (internationally)!

1-(B) - DATA. All the available radar data will be reexamined and reevaluated for accuracy and verification. It is believed, the country of Indonesia still has not contributed its radar data.

1-(C) - DATA. How accurately did the Inmarsat satellite scientists, mathematically determine the location of its two flight path arcs? One a northerly arc overland, and the other, a southerly arc over water, and placing the missing Boeing-777 in the South Indian Ocean and west of the continent of Australia. These two arcs (northerly and southerly), were mathematically determined by the six and one-half "handshakes," that occurred, between the geo-synchronous Inmarsat satellite and flight no. MH-370.

1-(D) - DATA. How accurately placed were the four pingings detected by the US Navy's "TPL" (towed pinger locator), towed by Australia's *Ocean Shield* search ship?

2 - *Bluefin-21* AUV limitations. Apparently, the four pingings detected were emitted, from very deep sea-floor beneath the Indian Ocean, below the 14,900', diving limitation of the *Bluefin-21* AUV (which prevents high-pressure implosion).

3 - Costs. The expanded search zone, projected to possibly cost sixty million dollars, may extend the duration of time needed to search for MH-370, by eight to twelve months. (See page 140.)

4 - Fundraising. Will a fourth nation join in sharing search costs? Or will individual companies, aircraft manufacturers, or satellite companies/operators help fund the search?

PART 53

The very necessary three-nation conference (Malaysia, China, Australia), held in Canberra, Australia, is convening today, Wednesday, May 7, 2014, and day no. 62.

The *Bluefin-21* AUV (a torpedo-shaped twenty-first century search drone) has executed eighteen missions mapping the sea floor in the prime search zone, covering approximately 154 square miles to two hundred square miles of underwater terrain. *Bluefin-21* AUV operational costs ranged from twenty-five thousand dollars to forty thousand dollars ($40,000) per day, depending on the type of challenge the never-before-mapped Indian Ocean presented. (See page 141.)

Unfortunately, *no* positive results were gained, and no Boeing-777 (flight 370) wreckage was found. *Yet* to this point in time.

A recently conducted CNN-ORC poll revealed:

A) 66% of people surveyed feel the search should continue.
B) 52% of people polled feel mechanical failure caused flight no. MH-370 to disappear and be categorized as still missing.
C) 57% of polled people feel terrorism or hostile governments were somehow involved in the disappearance of MA flight no. MH-370.
D) About one-half of the group polled, feel the Boeing-777 will one day be found.
E) About one-half of people in this poll, feel flight no. MH-370 will not be found.
F) 51% of people polled, feel the prime search zone is correct.

On the next day, which is Thursday, May 8, 2014, and day no. 63 of flight 370 still missing, the Canberra, Australia, three-nation conference, has the expert search team members from China, Malaysia, and Australia, beginning to review, and re-analyze, all facts pertaining to the loss of Malaysia Airlines flight no. MH-370.

Regarding the surviving family' members, these relatives all desire individual, personal copies of the data. These surviving relatives have requested all the data in writing from Malaysia.

The country of Malaysia remains the lead investigator, in the plight of the vanished Boeing-777, because Malaysia Airlines (ownership), is nationalized. The Malaysian nation owns Malaysia Airlines and the Boeing-777, that is missing flight no. MH-370.

PART 54

Swirling controversy is now emerging, on Friday, May 9, 2014 (EDT), and day no. 64 in the search for missing MA flight no. MH-370.

Under the interview of Pamela Brown, David Soucie is reporting that the Inmarsat satellite scientists are, indeed, very reputable scientists. The Inmarsat satellite northern arc data, as well as, the southern arc data, are both accurate and correct. However, it now appears, the analysis of the Inmarsat satellite data is being called into question, and may possibly be incorrect.

The problem is, why the Inmarsat satellite "handshakes" communications showed the Boeing-777 in motion, when in reality, it was parked and motionless on the ramp, at the Kuala Lumpur International Airport.

Later, in the evening, David Soucie's response points out, "Although the Inmarsat Satellite scientists are reputable, other minds must be allowed to rediagnose all the convergences of factual (reliable) data."

Summarily, Erin Burnett reports that, therefore, the big story has become the popular, consensual belief, seeming to indicate that possibly, the twenty-three countries (in total), searching for missing flight no. MH-370, and its 239 passengers and crew has spent two months, "looking in the wrong ocean."

PART 55

During day no. 65, which is Saturday, May 10, 2014 (EDT), Fredrika Whitfield, is reporting that today's focus of the three-nation convention (Malaysia, Australia, and China), being held in Canberra, Australia, is to reexamine the site of the first "pinging," detected and heard by the US Navy's "TPL" (towed pinger locator), which was towed by the Australian search ship *"Ocean Shield."*

Today, *Ocean Shield* has already left port and is en route to this first "pinging" zone, equipped with the *Bluefin-21* AUV.

On the next day, Sunday, May 11, 2014, which is day no. 66, the three-nation Canberra Conference is continuing in its mode, of its focus, on the reexamination of all factual data related to the disappearance of MA flight no. MH-370. Apparently, the only reliable and factual data consists of these three findings:

1) The six and one-half Inmarsat Satellite "handshakes" with Malaysia Airlines flight no. MH-370.
2) The available radar data from Malaysia and Thailand.
3) The four "pingings" detected and heard by the US Navy's "TPL," which was towed by the Australian search ship *Ocean Shield*.

PART 56

Peter Goelz, Former US NTSB managing director, conversing with Wolf on Monday, May 12, 2014 (EDT), and day no. 67, revealed three interesting and important components in the search for missing flight no. MH-370, now vanished for sixty-seven days. Peter pointed out that the three-nation Canberra Conference is now focusing on the variations(s) heard from the four "pingings," detected by the US Navy's "TPL."

Following are the three components revealed:

A) The two pingings detected on Saturday and Sunday, April 5 and April 6, 2014, pinged at a frequency of 37.5 KHZ, equaling the frequency and rate of actual "black box pingings."

B) Conversely, the other two "pingings," both heard on Tuesday, April 8, 2014, were discounted in their level(s) of frequency, equaling "pingings" detected at a frequency of only 27.5 KHZ, below that of actual "black box pingings," by 10 KHZ.

C) Another problem is that a portion of the four "pingings" detected, were emitted from much deeper water. So deep, that the *Bluefin-21* AUV, with its 14,900 foot safe diving depth limitation, may not have pinpointed actual aircraft wreckage, by not diving deeply enough for imaging.

Angus Houston, Australian search chief in the hunt to locate flight no. MH-370, says the search team must persist in its search for the location of the four "pingings," detected and heard, to its total conclusion.

This would indicate utilizing deeper diving AUVS. For example, the *Remus-6000* AUV, and/or, the *Orion* AUV. (See pages 140, 129, 127, 124, 123, 103, and 102.)

PART 57

At 1:45 PM, Tuesday, May 13, 2014 (EDT/EST), and day no. 68, Wolf is announcing, "Global plane tracking in real time is needed now." Peter Goelz is stating that Inmarsat Satellite Company, presently, has the capacity to track eleven thousand aircraft in flight concurrently.

ICAO (International Civil Aviation Organization) is now voting, in Montreal, Canada, on implementation of real-time aircraft-in-flight tracking. Tom Fuentes, fmr. asst. director, US FBI, says although real-time plane tracking is now needed (to prevent another vanished in-flight aircraft incident), his thirty years of experience in government service tells him: "There could be a five- to ten-year delay in its implementation."

Richard Quest, reporting from South Africa, is stating that Angus Houston still remains optimistic about "pinging" accuracy (in the finding of missing Malaysia Airlines flight no. MH-370).

PART 58

Today is day no. 69, Wednesday, May 14, 2014, and a delay has begun, in *Bluefin-21* AUV search operations, according to Ashleigh Banfield. Ashleigh is announcing, that there will be a three-, four-, or five-day interruption in the search for missing MA flight no. MH-370.

This present-delay is caused by a collision, that has just occurred, on-board the Australian search ship *Ocean Shield*. Apparently, *Bluefin-21* accidentally struck the AUV'S ship-board transponder, mounted on *Ocean Shield*, damaging a part on *Bluefin-21*.

The transponder provides communications between *Ocean Shield* and the *Bluefin-21* AUV, while diving on its essential sea-floor mapping mission(s), to locate missing flight no. MH-370, and its vanished 239 passengers and crew members.

The odyssey of the plight of missing MA flight no. MH-370 continues!

PART 59

Despite the sincere request, the plea, if you will, made eight days ago, by the members of the surviving families (of the vanished 239 human beings on board missing MA flight no. MH-370), for all search data in writing, they have not yet received the written data as of today. (See page 145.)

Today, day no. 70, Thursday, May 15, 2014, Mr. Hishammuddin Hussein, Malaysia's acting transportation minister, claims only Inmarsat Satellite Company has the Inmarsat raw data! In addition, the country of Malaysia, unaccustomed to, and inexperienced with, the investigation of major aircraft disaster(s), is seeking assistance from private contractors, in the search for missing MA flight no. MH-370.

Meanwhile, Malaysia Airlines Co. wants to pay fifty thousand dollars, to each of the surviving next of kin family members, of the 239 vanished passengers and crew of missing flight no. MH-370.

However, ICAO (International Civil Aviation Organization) says, the correct compensation should be $ 175,000. ICAO, during the previous two days, has reportedly, been voting to move forward with real-time in-flight aircraft tracking, so as to futuristically avert, and prevent another vanished in-flight aircraft. (Incidentally, ICAO's Montreal, Canada, Conference was convened so that another flight 370 cannot go missing, again).

Two and one-half hours after Mr. Hussein spoke, regarding the topic of release of Inmarsat Satellite raw data, requested by the surviving families eight days ago, more controversy arose. (See pages 152 and 145). Now, an Inmarsat Sat. Co. representative is stating, that the Inmarsat Raw Satellite data cannot be released, to the surviving family members, because the data is proprietary data. However, this Inmarsat representative also said the lead search investigator, Malaysia, does have the raw data, sought by the surviving families.

In review, whether or not the Inmarsat satellite raw data, derived from the analyses performed by Inmarsat Satellite scientists is still proprietary, Inmarsat Satellite Co. did release it to the country of Malaysia, the lead investigator.

Five more hours pass, when Erin Burnett consults with Miles O'Brien, pilot and aviation analyst, and Mr. Arthur Rosenberg, Esq. (attorney). So Erin raises a logical premise; precisely: It is possible Inmarsat's data may no longer be proprietary, in that, they (Inmarsat), have stated, that the data belongs to another. (Namely, Malaysia, the lead investigator).

Miles O'Brien replies, "Someone is lying", in reference to the raw data desired by the next of kin, and to be provided in written form to the surviving families' members (as they have requested).

Mr. Arthur Rosenberg states, that if the Malaysian authorities claim they do not possess the printed Inmarsat raw data, to hand to the surviving families' members, then it would be incumbent on Inmarsat Satellite Co. to release the satellite raw data publicly, including to the surviving family members.

Inmarsat Satellite Company claims their data has been examined by four separate sets of reputable scientists. Also, Australian search chief, Angus Houston, feels the INMARSAT satellite data is accurate and correct, yet says, the data should be open to both public and other scientific review.

PART 60

The on-going argumentative controversy, concerning the Inmarsat raw data, which established the prime search zone along arc no. 7, where the last one-half, of the six and one-half "handshake(s)" communications occurred, and the four "pingings" were "TPL" detected and heard, for *Bluefin-21* to dive, mapping the prime search zone's sea floors, is escalating dramatically today, Friday, May 16, 2014, day no. 71.

David Soucie is stating today that Malaysia has the raw data, but it is unaware of it. David, aligned with yesterday's opinion by Arthur Rosenberg, agrees it is incumbent on Inmarsat Satellite Co. to release its satellite raw data, but with the caveat of, excluding Inmarsat Company's proprietary intellectual property. However, should the data be released (and inaccuracies be uncovered), then, who would pay the tens of millions of dollars, already spent on searching, possibly the wrong ocean area, all possibly based on data inaccuracies and data analytical incorrectness. (See page 146.)

Mary Schiavo also agrees that Malaysia has the raw data, contained within the analyses of that raw data. Mary further states that both entities: "Can come clean and publicize it." Its publication (the Inmarsat raw data), would allow surviving family members to access, and read, the raw data they have requested. (See page 145.)

And furthermore, publication of the raw data would allow "other minds" to reanalyze the original findings, which possibly, could provide the development of a new triangulation for search purposes, thereby establishing a new target site to locate, the missing Boeing-777, MA flight no. MH-370. (See pages 137 and 127.)

Three and one-half hours later, Wolf assembles a three-person expert panel. Peter Goelz, and Renee Marsh, aviation analyst, both agree, that Malaysia has lost world credibility, by not releasing the Inmarsat raw data. Miles O'Brien says, nearly pleadingly, that the surviving families' members, and the world at large, wants to find out what happened to missing flight no. MH-370, plus locate the Boeing-777 wreckage (and its two "black boxes.")

Miles suggests an ideation, synonymously similar, to David Soucie's Earlier Ideation. (See pages 63 and 64). Miles's suggestion recommends Malaysia Airlines fuel and fly a Boeing-777 test flight, along the same way points (as indicated by the Inmarsat satellite "handshake(s)" data). This test flight may yield information, from which knowledge may be gained, perhaps providing that one clue, possibly, omitted from a paper analysis of the Inmarsat satellite data.

This is still a valid idea today day no. 71 or as earlier mentioned on day no. 27. (See pages 63 and 64.)

PART 61

Fredrika Whitfield is Broadcasting (on CNN), a report from Mr. Jim Clancy on Saturday, May 17, 2014, and day no. 72. Jim Clancy, correspondent, reports the current Inmarsat data is correct, according to Angus Houston, chief of Indian Ocean search operations. Next, Mary Schiavo and David Soucie are stating:

1) Inmarsat Satellite Co. did release the satellite data to Malaysia (in the form of numbered coordinates), by tracing and correlating MH-370'S flight path, using the six and one half "handshakes," between the Inmarsat Geo-Synchronous satellite and missing flight no. MH-370.

2) Malaysia is in charge of the search investigation. Therefore, the Malaysians are responsible for releasing data information. However, Malaysia has delegated search leadership to Australia's search chief, Angus Houston. Angus is also chief spokesman, in the search for missing flight no. MH-370, in the Southern Indian Ocean.

3) Mentioned also, is that Rob McCallum, underwater search expedition leader, and David Gallo, Woods-Hole Oceanographic Institute specialist, probably, have greater search knowledge, experience, and search equipment, than Malaysia possesses.

In regard to the Inmarsat raw data, Richard Quest, aviation analyst, states, "There are no reams and reams of raw data". The raw data consists of to and fro (back and forth), measurements, already furnished to Malaysia. Conversely, Malaysia claims there exists some international law, or policy, either hindering, or inhibiting, the release of data.

Miles O'Brien says to both Inmarsat and Malaysia, "Release the data, and release the analysis of the data, and release the algorithms (used in the analysis), of the data". (An algorithm is a mathematical procedure).

Later today, Mr. Paul Ginzberg, audio expert, is speaking on the topic of ocean noise, when, Miguel Marquez juxtaposes the question: "Were the pingings detected (by the 'TPL'), emitted from an aircraft 'black box'?" Paul's response, following, is threefold:

A) Actually, a dolphin can mimic a "black box ping,"
B) Low-pitch sound travels far, whereas, high-pitch sound does not,
C) On any given day, there are fifty thousand ships at sea, all creating noise(s).

PART 62

Brooke Baldwin is reporting, today, Monday, May 19, 2014 (EDT), day no. 74, that the Malaysian prime minister has made a statement regarding, the Inmarsat data. The Malaysia PM (prime minister) is saying, The Inmarsat satellite data will be released. The Malaysians want Inmarsat to release the data, now!

Next, Jeff Wise, aviation author, asks, "Why did the Inmarsat satellite 'handshakes' indicate a search zone in the southern Indian Ocean?" In response, Richard Quest says, Boeing Co. (manufacturer of the missing B-777), is heavily involved with the Malaysians, in the search for missing MA flight no. MH-370. Boeing Co. says, their patent protection indicates only certain Boeing Co. information can be released, nothing proprietary can be divulged. Jeff, still pessimistically, feels the mathematical algorithms derived from the six and one-half Inmarsat "handshakes" with flight 370, possibly led to an incorrect mathematical triangulation, that, in turn, led to mistakenly searching the Southern Indian Ocean.

Mr. Jules Jaffe, research oceanographer at Scripps Oceanographic Institute, basically states, it is not impossible for anything to have taken place, specifically by the captain's action(s), and/or the co-pilot's action(s), or a third party, possibly rescuing the Boeing-777 from crashing into land, due to the possibility of a mechanical failure, and/or impending disaster, by taking the Boeing-777 out over water namely, the Southern Indian Ocean.

* Jules also believes the best search method(s) would be deep-water AUVs, such as the *Remus-6000*, because of the sea-floor unevenness.

* Captain Shah's (captain of missing flight no. MH-370), brother-in-law says, "Captain Shah is not evil."
* Ms. Saima Mohsin, correspondent, is presently reporting, that the surviving family members, of the missing 239 passengers and crew, will now finally receive the data they have been desperately seeking, according to a joint statement from Inmarsat and Malaysia.
* Mr. K.S. Marendran, whose wife is a passenger on board missing MA flight no. MH-370, is communicating by telephone that he is glad, Inmarsat and the Malaysians are now in agreement on the release of the satellite data to the public.
* David Soucie is elated that the Inmarsat satellite data will be released but will not prove the Boeing-777 flew on the southern one-half of arc no. seven, as compared to flying the northern one-half (1/2) of arc no. seven. (See page 81.)
* Don Lemon is reporting, on the additional controversy, of a movie trailer (shown at the Cannes, France, Film Festival), titled *Vanishing Act* about missing MA flight no. MH-370.
* Former Malaysia PM Mathathir Mohammed feels MH-370 was commandeered by CIA - remote control.

PART 63

It is now 9:34 AM (EDT/US EST), on Tuesday, May 20, 2014, day no. 75, and Carol Costello is reporting, that Inmarsat Satellite Company is now officially announcing, it will release its raw data to the public. (Possibly bowing to international curiosity).

Six days later, on Monday, May 26, 2014 (EDT), Pamela Brown is reporting that Malaysia will release the Inmarsat satellite six and one-half "handshake(s)" data, tomorrow, on Tuesday, May 27, 2014, day no. 82. Pamela also states the last sea floor mapping mission search by the *Bluefin-21* AUV, will be happening on Wednesday, May 28, 2014.

David Soucie feels the missing Boeing-777 will, eventually, be found. The finding of missing flight no. MH-370 would certainly provide solace to the surviving families' members, of the vanished 239 passengers and crew on board MA flight no. MH-370.

Saima Mohsin is reporting that the Malaysian acting transportation minister, Hishasmuddin Hussein, is confirming that Malaysia will indeed release the Inmarsat satellite raw data, publicly, on Tuesday, May 27, 2014, tomorrow day no. 82.

PART 64

Happily, Inmarsat satellite raw data release day, for the general public of Planet Earth has finally arrived, today, Tuesday, May 27, 2014, and day no. 82!

Carol Costello is introducing Mr. Rupert Pearce, CEO (chief executive officer) of Inmarsat Satellite Company, of London, England. Rupert states his Inmarsat Satellite Company released a complete satellite report, and analysis, in a forty-seven-page document. He is confident his Inmarsat satellite scientists are correct, and that their data and analyses are both correct. Rupert also says it is Malaysia, that must make the satellite data, and analysis, public.

Richard Quest is reporting, that the Inmarsat Satellite Network is an eleven geo-stationary global satellite system. Richard states Inmarsat's calculations of the data within their analysis did establish a true model of the flight path of missing Malaysia Airlines flight no. MH-370.

This model held true when applied to other aircraft in flight, at the same time missing MA flight no. MH-370 was in flight, and including previous numerology from the same exact Boeing-777, that flew on March 8, 2014 (Malaysia Time Zone)/March 7, 2014 (US EST), AS MA flight no. MH-370.

The entire search in the Southern Indian Ocean was executed directly and exclusively according to the Inmarsat satellite data analysis.

Tom Forman, studying the forty-seven-page documented data analysis concluded two pages apply directly to missing flight no. MH-370, pages 40 and 41. These two pages identify Inmarsat's satellite no. 3 FI, as being the one satellite "handshaking" six and one-half times, with MA flight no. MH-370, during its final flight.

To obtain the probable flight path of missing flight no. MH-370, Inmarsat Satellite Company scientists, mathematically timing the six and one-half "handshakes," then, factoring-in frequency differences, or "versed frequency offset," as well as, the Doppler effect (also factored in), has established a "burst frequency (time) offset," thereby indicating an MH-370 southerly flight path, or route (heading of direction).

* The data analysis of the six and one half "handshakes," follows below:

Raw data	frequency	"burst frequency (time) offset"
1) 19:41	111	11500
2) 20:41	141	11740
3) 21:41	168	12780
4) 22:41	204	14540
5) 10:58	252	18040
6) 19:29	182	23000
6.5) 19:37	-2	49660
7) 00:19	(final seventh arc)	(no MH-370 "handshake" response)

To obtain a proper understanding of the above charted data, it is best interpreted by a physicist, mathematician, or both.

Incidentally, Mr. K. S. Marendran, husband of a missing passenger on board MH-370, is pleased. Later, Wolf is reporting, that, one of the surviving family members stated, the Inmarsat satellite data is not understandable, without an accompanying explanation of the analysis, derived from the data (itself).

Correspondent Renee Marsh, regarding the arcs ascertained from the Inmarsat satellite data analysis, is reporting, the marginal width of possible error of the Inmarsat-placed arcs locations, may/can be off-target, by a total sixty mile width (thirty miles east of arc/thirty miles west of arc).

There will be no underwater searching for a period of at least two months. Until private companies arrive at the search zone, equipped with better, deeper-diving search AUVs, approximately during the month of August 2014 or later.

Also, a Boeing-777 should not be reflown along the suspected flight path, because climatic, seasonal, and meteorological changes may yield a different timing of satellite "handshakes," differing from that of missing flight no. MH-370, on March 8, 2014 (Malaysia time zone)/March 7, 2014 (US EST), thereby proving nothing accurately or reliably.

PART 65

Today, during day no. 83, Wednesday, May 28, 2014 (EDT), Wolf announces, "A stunning setback! The US Navy is now on the record for discounting and disclaiming the accuracy of the four pings, that their TPL detected!" Apparently, underwater signals detected may not have been emitted from "black boxes." Mr. Michael Dean, US Navy, is stating the four "pingings" detected may have come from the Australian search ship *Ocean Shield*.

Peter Goelz, is speaking about addressing the frequencies of a portion of the four pingings detected, having incorrect frequencies, than the 37.5 KHZ, actually emitted from real "black boxes." (See page 148-B.)

And then, Renee Marsh, aviation analyst, reminds all of us interested, that the four pingings were not able to be reacquired. (See page 78.)

Angus Houston continues to reinforce the notion, that the four pingings detected were not emitted from nature, rather that they were man-made, generated signals.

However, the slim chance remains, that one underwater hydrophone station (of eleven such hydrophone stations), might have heard the Boeing-777 impacting the ocean water, west of the continent of Australia.

Also, today, day no. 83, marked the final sea floor mapping mission of the *Bluefin-21* AUV submersible, concluding a grand total, sea floor mapped search area of 329 sq. mi.

Unfortunately, so far, the *Bluefin-21* AUV (limited by its safe-diving maximum depth, of 14,900 feet), *has not* located the missing Boeing-777, known as MA flight no. MH-370.

The *Bluefin-21* AUV was originally first deployed on Monday, April 14, 2014, day no. 39. Its final searching dive, mapping the seafloor of the prime search zone today day no. 83, Wednesday, May 28, 2014, equals exactly a forty-five-day duration (around the clock = 24/7), of highly technical diving and mapping by the operational crew of scientists, mechanics, and technologists who really were and are a dedicated group of humanitarians, searching deep and dangerous, uncharted sea floor areas of the Indian Ocean, for the unfortunate and vanished 239 human occupants of MA flight no. MH-370. (Refer to page 141 and see pages 93 and 94.)

PART 66

Anchorwoman Ms. Ana Cabrera is in contact presently with Will Ripley, today, Thursday, May 29, 2014, and day no. 84. Will is now verifying the US Navy's report, discounting the veracity of the four pingings detected by their "TPL" (towed pinger locator), as false signals.

Later today, David Soucie, conversing with Brooke Baldwin, is now stating, that because the US Navy admits the four pings detected by their "TPL" have no veracity, then the Inmarsat satellite data remains the only reliable information indicating the possible flight path, of missing Malaysia Airlines flight no. MH-370, correctly.

Concerning the upcoming phase two search to find still missing MA flight no. MH-370, the new search field has been expanded to a thirty-four thousand square mile area. The necessary search contracts will be awarded to private contractors, having the ability to deploy specialized deeper-diving AUVs.

The southern end of Inmarsat analytical arc no. seven is located in the southern hemisphere of our Earth, in the South Indian Ocean, possibly where MH-370 ran out of fuel.

PART 67

During the discussion and examination of all factual evidence available, in the search for the mysteriously disappeared flight MH-370, Cable News Network (CNN), announces, "Back to square one." Anchorwoman Ms. Randi Kaye consults with five experts on six relevant points pertaining to the vanished Boeing-777, on day no. 86, today, Saturday, May 31, 2014:

1) David Gallo, Woods-Hole Oceanographic Institute, states: "This next search phase will take a long time" (probably meaning months or years).

2) Paul Ginzberg, audio expert, is saying "pings" were heard, however, the *Bluefin-21* AUV could not dive deeply enough (to pinpoint B-777 debris).

3) Jeff Wise, author, is stating he does not know why the four pings behaved differently, at varying frequencies, and he is (as we are) baffled.

4) Mr. David Mearns of Blue Water Recoveries, says that one cannot discount the fact (the horror) that a Boeing-777 with 239 people is missing.

5) Mr. Daniel Rose, attorney, claims, without positive search results that the surviving family members are upset. (With 239 relatives missing.)

6) Lastly, Randi adds, "Only the Chinese Navy continually keeps searching, the Southern Indian Ocean because over 150 Chinese passengers were on board missing Malaysia Airlines flight no. MH-370."

Three days later, however, Tuesday, June 3, 2014, day no. 89, David Soucie has an important announcement, during an interview with John Berman and Michaela Peireira. David is now announcing, that an underwater hydrophone detected a noise, about the same time that the disappearance of missing flight no. MH-370 occurred.

Later, on day no. 89, Wolf is reporting Australian researchers have revealed they detected, and actually heard, a dull thud-sounding noise, at about the same time, of/as, the disappearance of missing flight no. MH-370. Although, their hydrophone array is positioned three thousand miles west of the Australian continent.

Peter Goelz tells Wolf, the Inmarsat satellite six and one half "handshakes" data is still presently remaining, the most reliable information possessed by search teams. Wolf replies in agreement, that without the Inmarsat six and one-half "handshakes" data then we (the search teams), would be: "Back to square one."

PART 68

Negotiations are presently ongoing, concerning the awarding of new search contracts to private deep-ocean water search contractors. Also, today, Monday, June 9, 2014, day no. 95, it is now being revealed and reported, that the phase two underwater search for missing flight MH-370 will be shifted to a new location, based on factoring in new fuel quantity totals and fuel-burn-rate ratios (mileage), information on MH-370, to more precisely match, the reexamination and reanalysis of the Inmarsat Satellite company's six and one-half "handshakes" data.

Tonight, on day no. 95, Pamela Brown is reporting that five families, of all the surviving family members of the missing 239 crew and passengers on board vanished MA flight no. MH-370, are now presently seeking five million dollars in donations. The five million dollars will be used to assist in the search for the missing Boeing-777. And amazingly, to reward anyone who comes forward (with secret information), as to what happened to the aircraft, and its missing 239 passengers and crew and also the missing aircraft's present location.

PART 69

Nine days pass when on Wednesday, June 18, 2014, day no. 104, Brooke Baldwin is now reporting a new search site is being announced, located hundreds of miles southwest of the original search site. Brooke then interviews Jeff Wise, who is stating, the new Inmarsat satellite data analysis has been mathematically determined, and that the following three factors were considered:

1) The original six and one-half Inmarsat "handshakes" data (with MH-370),
2) The navigation of the missing Boeing-777 (direction and altitudes),
3) The rate of fuel-burn, indicating the aircraft's mileage range (thereby, therefore).

Five more days elapse, and on day no. 109, Monday, June 23, 2014, Carol Costello is stating that Australia is considering a new search site for MH-370, said to be located hundreds of kilometers south of the original prime search zone, where the "TPL" detected four pingings and the AUV *Bluefin-21* mapped the sea floor for forty-five days. (See pages 165 and 141.)

Incidentally, Mary Schiavo agrees with Australia, about MH-370's altitude discrepancies, being verified by radar data, and Inmarsat satellite data.

Renee Marsh, also is reporting, the new search location will be hundreds of miles southwest (SW) of the original prime search zone, and that the alleged flight path of missing MA flight no. MH-370, involves a 1,600-mile arc, intersecting near Inmarsat (southernmost) arc no. seven. (See pages 81 and 162.)

PART 70

Again, *the profundity of the plight of missing flight no. MH-370 deepens,* relative to more controversial assumptions emerging at this time.

At 5:51 AM (EDT/EST) of Thursday, June 26, 2014, and day no. 112 in the saga of the disappearance of flight no. MH-370, Christine Romans is now reporting that the missing Boeing-777 apparently may have been flying on its automatic pilot, when possibly, it ran out of (Jet-A) Fuel. And the new search area will be farther south.

The new search area encompasses sixty thousand square kilometers equaling 23,000 square miles, or an area the size of West Virginia (USA). It continues along the same arc no. seven, indicated by Inmarsat Satellite Co.'s data, but farther south/southwest. (See page 81.) The new search area is a consequence of factoring together all the considerations involved and including: A) computerized automatic-pilot flight path, B) regulated fuel-feed burn-rate at high-altitude, to obtain maximum range/distance (an aircraft experiences less drag resulting in reduced fuel burn, at a higher altitude, such as 37,000 feet because of lessened atmospheric density), and also, C) the Boeing-777 glide-ratio(s), with engines flamed out. (See pages 86, 87, and 131.)

Also, the new search zone (the size of West Virginia) will be thoroughly sea-floor mapped with sonar, prior to underwater searching, beginning with AUVs. (See pages 102, 103, 123, and 124.)

Ms. Renee Marsh is now reporting, investigators have assumed the missing Boeing-777 may have flown its final five hours of flight as *a ghost ship!* They are surmising the Boing-777 flew on automatic pilot, with both the flight cabin (cockpit), and passenger cabin, deprived of oxygen! This condition is known as *hypoxia*. It is defined medically as a lack of oxygen to the body and/or brain.

Peter Goelz, Fmr. NTSB managing director, states, "An information vacuum (void) cannot exist in aviation." So Richard Quest, aviation analyst, explains that the four pingings, detected by the US Navy's "TPL," were erroneously heard. Instead, it seems the "TPL" may have been hearing the Australian search ship *Ocean Shield*, while it towed its "TPL." Next, Richard speculates flight no. MH-370 may have spiraled downward, out of control, into the Indian Ocean.

However, the basic law of hydraulics and hydro-dynamics states: "Liquids behave as solids." Meaning, a downward spiraling, out-of-control, Boeing-777 impacting into an ocean surface, would generate forces equivalent to slamming into concrete, considering the enormous weight and airspeed of said Boeing-777.

Therefore, such a spiraling downward, out-of-control, Indian Ocean surface impact would have caused a tremendous airframe break apart, and the releasing of the resulting floating wreckage/debris. Insulation, seat cushions, and some aircraft composite materials float. Unfortunately, *no floating Boeing-777 wreckage or debris was ever found!*

Note: The author's opinion follows:

By contrast, the possibility may exist, of an automatically-piloted aircraft descent, with an appropriate glide-ratio angle of attack, onto the Indian Ocean surface (allowing the aircraft to ditch, near-horizontally, onto the ocean surface), and then sink intact, by gradually submerging, without airframe implosion, due to equalized pressurization (internally/externally), as water slowly infiltrates the (barely damaged) fuselage, and eventually reaching the sea floor, of the deep Indian Ocean. Tragically, and furthermore, it is unknown, if whether passengers and/or crew were unconscious?! (Please see pages 86 and 87.)

Today, day no. 112, 7:42 PM (EDT/EST), the official investigation report is released. It speaks directly to the location, within the southern Indian Ocean, where the missing Boeing-777 may have come to rest on the sea floor, in line with the Inmarsat Satellite Company analytical arc no. seven, and, in direct linear correlation with the Inmarsat six and one-half "satellite handshakes" with MH-370. (See pages 81 and 162.)

However, today's investigation report intentionally does not, directly or indirectly, answer the important aviation industry question of why, and how, a well-seasoned and highly-experienced pilot, of the caliber of Captain Zahari Shah, would ditch into the sea! (Or First Officer (co-pilot) Fariq Hamid.)

PART 71

Three additional days have elapsed, when aviation analyst and author David Soucie theorizes why and how no floating B-777 wreckage was found. (And supporting this author's earlier postulated hypothesis). (See page 173.)

David states today, Sunday, June 29, 2014 (EDT), day no. 115, if the flight cabin (cockpit) lost pressurization while coinciding with reserve oxygen bottle problems then the flight crew (before losing consciousness), may have engaged the Boeing-777'S automatic pilot. Assuming, if, the automatic pilot's program included a gradual descent from flight altitude, then the missing Boeing-777 may have landed intact onto the Indian Ocean surface. Over time, as ocean water gains entry into the fuselage, the aircraft would sink to the sea-floor intact! And the many atmospheres of pressure (encountered at sea-floor depths of fifteen thousand feet to twenty thousand feet would equalize, internally matching externally). And thereby relegating the fuselage's integrity, remaining in virtually good condition! (See pages 68, 69 and 173.)

This perspective would explain why no break-up occurred, hence no floating wreckage! (See pages 86 and 87.)

PART 72

Now, after an additional eight weeks and four days have elapsed, Jeff Wise, author, is stating that Malaysia Airlines tried to contact flight no. MH-370 via two satellite phone calls, on two separate satellite phone systems. The two satellite phones on board MH-370 were working, yet no communication(s) were established, according to Jeff, while speaking with John Berman, on Thursday morning, August 28, 2014 (EDT), and day no. 175 since MH-370 vanished.

Later, during the early afternoon, aviation analyst Renee Marsh, consulting with Wolf, is reporting, that MH-370 did turn south earlier, based on the two satellite phone calls. Apparently, it is unclear why this indicates that MA no. MH-370 may have turned south earlier.

So therefore, this means the upcoming phase two search will focus farther south, along the Inmarsat satellite (analytical), final arc no. 7, raw data coordinate 00.19. (See page 162.)

This is where the one-half handshake (of the six and one-half "handshakes"), was not returned, by not answering with a (total) seventh response, from flight no. MH-370 (7 - ½ = 6 ½). (See pages 162 and 81.)

At this time, a few search areas remain. The prime search zone is smaller, at least fifteen miles in length. And the largest search area is 150 miles long.

Specifically, one of the two satellite phone calls, from our Earth to flight no. MH-370 is re-positioning the underwater search zone, more to the south of Inmarsat analytical southern arc no. seven. The northernmost area of southern arc no. seven, is located west of Perth, Australia. (See page 81.)

The northernmost area of southern arc no. seven is south of our equator.

The new phase two search for MH-370 will/may last one year, and cost forty-eight million dollars. The phase two search should commence in approximately three or four weeks. Underwater sea floor mapping with sonar is already being done, in preparation for the beginning of the phase two search for missing MH-370. Meanwhile, the investigation into the disappearance of MA flight no. MH-370 continues, with further analysis of interviews with involved people, and preexisting factual information.

Unfortunately, two days later, on Saturday, August 30, 2014, and day no. 177 of the vanished B-777, Malaysia Airlines is now announcing that they have lost one hundred million dollars, during their second quarter, and have laid off six thousand employees or 30 percent of their workforce.

PART 73

Tom Forman is reporting today, Saturday, October 4, 2014, and day no. 212 in the quest to find missing flight no. MH-370, that in preparation to commence the phase two hunt, for MA no. MH-370, sonar-equipped ships have mapped sixteen thousand square miles of Indian Ocean sea floor, up until now.

A portion of this sea floor mapped is named "Broken Ridge." It consists of mountains, valleys, plunging canyons, and crumbling volcanoes. Tom also states there is greater certainty as to where, along Inmarsat southern arc no. seven, the vanished Boeing-777, probably ran out of fuel (Jet-A kerosene).

The phase two search should officially commence, in two days, on Monday, October 6, 2014, which would be day no. 214, or greater than thirty weeks, since Malaysia Airlines Flight no. MH-370 disappeared.

The phase two search will employ underwater towed submersibles, such as the *Orion*. Search "mother" control ships will pull the submersible(s) with cables, having lengths as long as four miles, to accommodate ocean depths of twenty thousand feet! (See pages 102, 103, 123, and 124).

PART 74

Finally, the phase two search for missing Malaysia Airlines flight no. MH-370 is now beginning, today, Monday, October 6, 2014, on day no. 214! The vanished Boeing-777 disappeared completely from all sight and sound on our planet Earth, 214 days ago, definitely under mysterious and bewildering circumstances, on Saturday, March 8, 2014 (Malaysia Time Zone)/Friday, March 7, 2014 (US EST).

Malaysia time zone is twelve hours earlier than United States Eastern Standard Time (US EST) Zone. (See page 23.)

Please keep in mind, when flight no. MH-370 received Kuala Lumpur tower clearances for taxiing (12:32 AM) and take-off (12:42 AM), it was Malaysia time zone. But simultaneously at the same precise moment, it was twelve hours earlier, 12:32/12:42 PM (EST), in the USA, as compared to Malaysia. Therefore, because of Earth calendar time: 12:32/12:42 AM, SATURDAY, MARCH 8, 2014 (Malaysia Time Zone), equals 12:32/12:42 PM, Friday, MARCH 7, 2014 (US EST). Twelve hours later (in Malaysia) equals one day earlier in the USA!

Good news! Three search-ships have already been dispatched, and now have completed the heart-pounding, white-knuckled voyage, thrashing their way across the dangerous surface of the vast Indian Ocean, to arrive at their targeted, and reanalyzed, searching site(s)!

The Three Search-Ships (Deployed) Are Named:

A) *Discovery*, now on scene at new search zone,
B) *Equator*, now on scene at new search zone,
C) *Go Phoenix*, now on scene at new search zone.

And the *Echo* is the cable–towed sonar exploration device, capable of accommodating Indian Ocean depths of twenty thousand feet, that is being towed by the above-listed trio of "controlling mother search ships," in the hunt to locate the vanished Boeing-777, including its 239 missing occupants, known internationally as disappeared MA flight no. MH-370.

The *Echo* exploration submersible probably features design elements comparable to those engineered into the *Orion* submersible. Including the three segmented tow cable of which one portion provides live streaming for sending video imagery and other data immediately up to the operations crew on board the "mother control search vessel," pulling the submersible. (See pages 102, 103, 123, 124, and 129.)

The *Echo* moves at a speed of four knots per hour, compared to *Bluefin-21*s forward speed of one knot per hour, possibly quadrupling searching rate, speed, and time.

The phase two search mission to find missing MA no. MH-370 has a new Australian search chief, named Mr. Martin Dolan. Martin is stating, the new phase two search area is located in an extremely remote portion of the Indian Ocean about 1,200 miles west of Australia. However, he also believes his new ship sonar scanned, search map/chart(s) are more accurate than those used four to five months ago, during the phase one search, utilizing the *Bluefin-21* AUV.

Miles O'Brien is saying, "If we keep looking, then we will find missing flight 370!" Later, Miles adjusts his narrative by adding an intriguing, disclaiming caveat, saying, if or when MA no. MH-370 is found, the mystery of why MH-370 vanished, may not be solved, conclusively or definitively.

Nonetheless, Ms. Sarah Bajc, girlfriend of missing MH-370 passenger Phillip Wood, surely continues hoping for Malaysia Airlines flight no. MH-370 to be found.

And so, the dedicated humanitarians aboard the trio of search ships, *Discovery*, *Equator*, and *Go Phoenix*, ply forwardly ahead with the submersible *Echo* (see page 180), in their quest to hunt and find the vanished Boeing-777, MH-370 . . .

PART 75

How odd, unusual, is it, that 239 Earthlings would climb aboard a human-designed, engineered, and built human flying machine, as normal, to travel to another region of our planet Earth, daring to fly up into the unknown of "the wild, blue yonder", but vanish!

The occurrence of such a disappearance seems a reminder of the adage: "God giveth, and God taketh away." God giving is a blessing, and oddly, God taketh away, may possibly be another blessing, disguised in a reverse way.

In the vastness of our known and unknown universe, it seems our Earth is known and unknown.

In the vastness of our universe, it seems evident that all we Earthlings on our planet Earth, are only but ants, within the big picture of our universe.

But very intelligent, and curious, Earthly human ants! Fortunately, *hope springs daily, living eternally!*

The end.

EPILOGUE

Dear reader:

Should you be desirous of a hypothetical/theoretical solution to the mysterious disappearance of Malaysia Airlines flight no. MH-370, then at your discretion, please turn this page to reveal a map, where I the author have charted the location where I have determined MA flight no. MH-370, may have arrived at its final resting place.

RD, author and artist

The World

NORTHERN ARC #7

ARC #7

AUTHOR'S HYPOTHETICAL
MH-370'S LOCATION

PHASES I+II
SEARCH ZONES

Atlas Legen

MH-370 UPDATE

July 8th, 2018

Vanished Malaysia Airlines Flight No. MH-370, disappeared on/since March 8th, 2014, to July 8th, 2018, so far. By any Calendar, 4 Years and 4 Months, so far. After both Phase 1 and Phase 2 Searches, plus, including the privately-funded Phase 3 Search, which officially concluded on Monday, May 28th, 2018, (U.S. Memorial Day Holiday), by The Private Search Contractors. All three (3) Searches inspected The Indian Ocean Surface, and especially and particularly the sea-floor of The Indian Ocean, in the areas where the three (3) Searches targeted their hunt(s). To the chagrin of Our Planet Earth's Populace, the huge Boeing-777 remains missing, following a combined, but consecutive, 4 Year and 4 Month searching by dedicated humanitarians, seeking the vanished 239 passengers and crew, both "Black Boxes", and The Boeing-777 Airframe Itself. Unfound for 4 Years and 4 Months, so far.

However, approximately A Dozen Fragments or Pieces have washed-up onto Reunion Island, and some, from Madagascar - to - Mozambique, Africa.

Unfortunately, all 239 occupants, both "Black Boxes", as well as, the Boeing-777 Airframe, remain missing and unaccounted for, 4 years and 4 months after, "The Final Flight Of MH-370."

R.D., Author/ Artist.

ADDENDUM: NOTE

The addendum following has nothing directly connected to or involved with, the preceding story, written about and named:

The Mysterious Final Flight Of MH-370.

The Most Fascinating, Anomalous Mystery Disappearance in A Century - Since The Sinking Of The TITANIC.

An Enlightened Observer's Diary of The Chronological, Historical Facts, Surrounding The Tragic Loss of Missing Malaysia Airlines Flight No. MH-370,
a Boeing-777-200 series.

Including, "Addendum: M.A. Flight No. MH-17".

Robert Dominguez, Author/Artist, Reg.
Copyright: December 12, 2014.

ADDENDUM:
MA FLIGHT NO. MH-17
DISASTER

At 11:20 AM (US EDT/EST), on Thursday, July 17, 2014, Cable News Network (CNN) is now reporting "breaking news." Mr. John Berman is now stating that Reuter's News Agency is presently reporting: a jet aircraft has just been shot down to our Earth from an altitude of thirty-three thousand feet by an anti-aircraft missile! With no survivors alive! (33,000 Feet = 10 KM = 10,000 meters of altitude!)

The aircraft in question turned out to be Malaysia Airlines flight no. MH-17, another Boeing-777 MA flight no. MH-17, departing from Amsterdam, the Netherlands, had a destination point of Kuala Lumpur, Malaysia, and then was to continue on to other Asian final destinations. It was also reported the missile that targeted MA flight no. MH-17 was a Russian-designed BUK anti-aircraft, track-driven, military defensive weapon (radar-directed, rather than heat-seeking).

On board MA flight no. MH-17, were 298 people in total, including a fifteen-member Malaysian flight crew. So therefore, there were 283 paying passengers.

There were 192 Netherlands citizens, with one possessing dual citizenship, in the Netherlands and the United States. Twenty-eight Malaysian passengers between one to two dozen Australian passengers, and the remainder of the victims on the passenger manifest were from other countries. So unfortunately, there were no survivors from approximately a dozen nations, whose citizenry comprised the complete passenger and crew manifest(s), on board the targeted Malaysia Airlines Flight no. MH-17.

Apparently, pro-Russian separatists downed the MA flight no. MH-17, probably incorrectly believing, mistakenly, the aircraft may have been a Ukrainian AN-26 cargo plane. Malaysia Airlines flight no. MH-17, in fact, overflew an active war zone, having a thirty-two thousand foot altitude restriction.

The world population strongly feels there was Russian involvement possibly. Interestingly, the BUK anti-aircraft missile was launched by perhaps a four-man crew, without the assistance of the accompanying wide-scan radar vehicle, whose function is to interpret transponder transmitting communication(s), which differentiate civilian aircraft from military aircraft.

Since and because the Malaysia Airlines flight no. MH-17 (a Boeing-777), was flying at an altitude of thirty-three thousand feet (one thousand feet above the thirty-two thousand–foot warzone altitude restriction, over the Eastern Ukrainian warzone), all the circumstances beg the question to be asked: WHY?

This wreckage site of the downed Malaysia Airlines flight no. MH-17 is on land. When aviation disaster investigators finally arrived on site, they discovered that the fuselage had many punctures. Apparently, these punctures were caused by an exploding warhead, piercing the fuselage in flight, and thereby compromising its integrity, causing it to fall out of the sky, thirty-three thousand feet to the ground of our earth on impact!

Eventually, a majority of the victims that were able to be recovered, were transported and returned to the Netherlands for medical examination(s) and forensic identification(s).

The Netherlands authorities treated the bodies of the victims, ceremoniously, with great pomp and circumstance. However, some victims remain missing, yet to be found!

Certainly, the MA flight no. MH-17 aircraft disaster may have contributed to the loss, by Malaysia Airlines of $100,000,000 in their second quarter, plus the six thousand employees lay off.

This, is in addition to the still missing MA flight no. MH-370, which mysteriously vanished 132 days earlier, on March 8, 2014 (Malaysia Time Zone)/March 7, 2014 (US EST).

Again, this particular incident/accident (MH-17), resulted in the death(s) of all 298 passengers and crew on-board. Malaysia Airlines flight no. MH-17, unfortunately had no survivors.

The end of addendum.

© Reg. Copyright

December 12, 2014,

Robert Dominguez, author/artist,

BIBLIOGRAPHY

- Broadcast: Cable News Network (CNN), an American-based cable TV broadcaster of newsworthy events and having a cadre of reputable journalists and reliable sources internationally located/dispatched.
- Newspaper(s): *Wall Street Journal, USA Today, England's Daily Mirror, Miami Herald, Fort Lauderdale News & Sun-Sentinel,* provided verification(s) for the chronological, historical facts of *The Mysterious Final Flight Of MH-370,* Registered Copyright December 12, 2014, a.k.a. *Chapter 2: The Mysterious Final Flight of MA No. MH-370,* Reg © December 12, 2014 by Robert Dominguez, sole author/artist, all rights reserved, written and contained herein.
- Companies, corporations, and governmental agencies: Inmarsat Satellite Company of UK; Boeing Company, an American aircraft manufacturer with diverse projects specializing in space exploration and space-related equipment and associated with US NASA; DOT = US Department of Transportation; FAA = US Federal Aviation Administration; NTSB = US National Transportation Safety Board; Malaysia Airlines Co. of Malaysia, SE Asia; Phoenix International Company of USA; United States Navy; Australian Navy; Chinese Navy; and Bangladesh Navy, South Asia.

BIBLIOGRAPHICAL SOURCES

(In order of appearance)

1) Captain Zahari Shah: Captain and Commander of Malaysia Airlines Flight no. MH-370, on March 8, 2014 (Malaysia Time Zone)/March 7, 2014 (US EST). At Kuala Lumpur International Airport, Malaysia, Captain Shah, in communication with The KL control tower, obtained clearance(s) for A 12:32 AM taxiing (Malaysia Time Zone), and a 12:42 AM (MTZ), departure take off, then flew, the now missing Boeing-777.

2) First Officer Fariq Hamid: Co-pilot in the Cockpit of Malaysia Airlines Flight no. MH-370.

3) Mr. Phillip Wood: One American Passenger that flew on MH-370 on March 8/7, 2014.

4) Mr. John Berman: CNN Anchorman.

5) Mr. Wolf Blitzer: CNN Anchorman.

6) Mr. Tom Forman: CNN Virtual Imaging Journalist.

7) Mr. Richard Quest: CNN Aviation Analyst.

8) Mr. Jake Tapper: CNN Anchorman.

9) Mr. Michael Goldfarb: Former FAA Chief-of-Staff.

10) Mr. Peter Goelz: Former NTSB Managing Director.

11) Mr. Jim Sciutto: CNN International Correspondent.

12) Mr. Patrick Smith: Aviation Analyst.

13) Mr. Keith Wolzinger: Boeing-777 Pilot.

14) Mr. Don Lemon: CNN Anchorman.

15) Mr. Brian Todd: CNN Correspondent.

16) Ms. Brooke Baldwin: CNN Anchorwoman.

17) Mr. Chad Myers: CNN Meteorologist.

18) Ms. Erin Burnett: CNN Anchorwoman.

19) Mr. Miles O'Brien: Licensed Pilot, Aviation Analyst, Chief Science Correspondent at PBS, (Public Broadcasting System), and previously at CNN.

20) Ms. Ashleigh Banfield: CNN Anchorwoman.

21) Mr. Ed Lavandera: CNN Correspondent.

22) Mr. David Soucie: Fmr. DOT/FAA Accident Investigator, Aviation Analyst, and Author.

23) Mr. Martin Savidge: CNN Correspondent.

24) Mr. Mitchell Casada (Quesada): Boeing-777 Simulator Instructor/Pilot Trainer.

25) Mr. Nicholas Mallos: Oceanographer, and Gyre-Expert, The Ocean Conservancy Group.

26) Mr. Mark Weiss: Boeing-777 Captain.

27) Mr. Tom Fuentes: Fmr. US FBI Asst. Director, and, Investigator-In-Charge.

28) Mr. Ryan Abernathy: Columbia University Academic.

29) Mr. Les Abend: Boeing-777 Captain.

30) Mr. Leo Romejin: Satellite Imaging Analyst.

31) Mr. Ian MacDonald: Ocean Gyre Expert.

32) Ms. Rosa Flores: CNN Correspondent.

33) Ms. Colleen Keller: Metron Inc., Senior Analyst.

34) Mr. Will Ripley: CNN Correspondent (Reporting from Australia).

35) Mr. Anderson Cooper: CNN Anchorman.

36) Mr. William Marks: Commander of US Navy's *Blue Ridge* search-ship.

37) Mr. Rob McCallum: Professional Underwater SEARCH Expedition Leader/Specialist.

38) Mr. Keith Masback: CEO of Geo-Spatial Intelligence Foundation.

39) Dr. Sanjay Gupta: Neurosurgeon.

40) Ms. Shah: Daughter of Captain Shah, who flew MH-370 March 8, 2014 (Malaysia Time Zone/March 8, 2014 (US EST).

41) Ms. Sara Sidner: CNN Correspondent.

42) Mr. David Funk: Retired Northwest Airlines Pilot.

43) Ms. Mary Schiavo: Former US DOT Chief of Accident Investigation.

44) Mr. David Gallo: Woods-Hole Oceanographic Institute AUV Expert.

45) Mr. Chuck Hagel: US Secretary of Defense.

46) Mr. Tim Taylor: Tiburon Sub(mersible)s Co., underwater search expert.

47) Mr. Kit Darby: Fmr. United Airlines Pilot, and, kitdarby.com President.

48) Mr. William J. McGee: Author of *Eight Chief Reasons for Aircraft Accidents*.

49) Mr. Bill Schofield: First Aviation "black box" Innovator.

50) Ms. Kyung Lau: CNN Correspondent.

51) Mr. Marcus Eriksen: "Five Gyres Institute" Executive Director.

52) Ms. Renee Marsh: CNN Aviation Analyst and Transportation Consultant.

53) Ms. Carol Costello: CNN Anchorwoman.

54) Ms. Paula Stewart: CNN Correspondent.

55) Ms. Christine Dennison: CNN Correspondent.

56) Mr. Arnold Carr: Aviation Analyst.

57) Ms. Deborah Feyerick: CNN Correspondent.

58) Mr. Mathew Chance: CNN Correspondent.

59) Mr. Tony Abbott: Australia Prime Minister (PM).

60) Mr. Najib Razak: Malaysia Prime Minister (PM).

61) Mr. Jim Tilmon: Retired pilot and captain.

62) Mr. Michael Kay: British RAF Pilot, Lieutenant Colonel, and Mathematician.

63) Mr. Jeff Wise: Author of *Extreme Fear*.

64) Mr. Angus Houston: Ret. Chief Air Marshall, and head of MH-370 Joint Agency SEARCH.

65) Ms. Jennifer Gray: CNN Meteorologist.

66) Ms. Fredrika Whitfield: CNN Anchorwoman.

67) Mr. Don Ginzburg/Ginzberg: Audio Sciences Expert.

68) Mr. Thomas Altshuler: Vice President (VP) of Teledyne Company.

69) Mr. David Stupples: Engineer, City University, London, England.
70) Mr. Bill Nye: Former Boeing Aircraft Engineer.
71) Ms. Kyra Phillips: CNN Anchorwoman.
72) Ms. Jean Casarez: Attorney/CNN Correspondent.
73) Mr. Robert "Bob" Ballard: First explorer to find *Titanic* (circa 1985).
74) Mr. Chesley "Sully" Sullenberger III: Captain, A320, who successfully landed on NYC's Hudson River, without any engines running and forever named "The Miracle on the Hudson" (as all passengers and crew deplaned physically unscathed)!
75) Mr. Alan Diehl: Author, *Aircraft Disasters*.
76) Mr. Van Gurley: Metron Inc. Scientific Solutions.
77) Mr. Paul Ginzberg: Audio Expert.
78) Mr. Bob Francis: NTSB, former vice chairman.
79) Ms. Candy Crowley: Journalist/CNN Correspondent.
80) Ms. Michaela Peireira: CNN Anchorwoman.
81) Ms. Pamela Brown: CNN Correspondent.
82) Mr. David Kelly: "*BLUEFIN-21*" AUV Engineer/Phoenix International Company.
83) Mr. Chris Cuomo: CNN Anchorman and Journalist.
84) Mr. Murtugudde: Oceanic Scientist.
85) Ms. Christine Romans: CNN Correspondent.
86) Ms. Sylvia Earle: National Geographic Society.
87) Mr. Richard Gillespie: Aviation Analyst.
88) Mr. David Wise: Science Writer.
89) Mr. Arthur Rosenberg: Aviation Attorney.
90) Mr. David Mattingly: CNN Correspondent.
91) Mr. Phil Nuyjen: Submersible Manipulator Originator.
92) Mr. Fabien Cousteau: Oceanographer.
93) Mr. Miguel Marquez: CNN Correspondent.
94) Ms. Erin McLaughlin: CNN Correspondent.
95) Ms. Rosemary Church: CNN Anchorwoman.
96) Mr. Ken Christensen: Lieutenant Colonel/Aviation Consultant.
97) Mr. President Barack Obama: Two-term United States president (Jan. 20, 2009 to Jan. 20, 2017).

98) Mr. Albert Einstein: Physicist, author of *Special Theory Of Relativity* and *General Theory Of Relativity* and theorized "The 'Fabric' Of The Space-Time Continuum," whereby light rays bend around gravitational masses. A solar eclipse proved his theory correct.

99) Ms. Cheng Liping: The wife of a missing MA flight MH-370 Chinese passenger.

100) Ms. Liu Wanyi: The wife of a missing MA flight MH-370 Chinese passenger.

101) Mr. Steve Wallace: Former director of US FAA accident investigation.

102) Mr. Hishammuddin Hussein: Malaysia, Acting Transportation Minister.

103) Mr. Jim Clancy: CNN Correspondent.

104) Mr. Jules Jaffe: Scripps Oceanographic Institute Researcher.

105) Captain Shah's Brother-in-Law: See Page 156.

106) Ms. Saima Mohsin: CNN Correspondent.

107) Mr. K.S. Marendran: The Husband of a missing MA flight no. MH-370 passenger.

108) Mr. Mathathir Mohammed: Former Malaysia Prime Minister (PM).

109) Mr. Rupert Pearce: Chief Executive Officer (CEO) of Inmarsat Satellite Company.

110) Mr. Michael Dean: United States Navy.

111) Ms. Ana Cabrera: CNN Correspondent/Anchorwoman.

112) Ms. Randi Kaye: CNN Anchorwoman.

113) Mr. David Mearns: "Blue Water Recoveries."

114) Mr. Daniel Rose: Attorney.

115) Mr. Robert Dominguez: Author's "Indian Ocean Miracle" Opinion.

116) Mr. Martin Dolan: Phase two search New Australian chief.

117) Ms. Sarah Bajc: The girlfriend of a missing MA flight no. MH-370 American passenger.

118) Humanitarian searchers: All the good Samaritan, humanitarian searchers hunting daily for vanished MA flight MH-370,
its 239 still missing souls, two "black boxes," and disappeared
B-777 physical airframe, during both, the phase one (#1)
search, and, the phase two (#2) search, and, the phase three
(#3) privately-funded search, by aircraft, ocean-surface ships,
underwater sea-floor AUV(s) and by satellite(s).

ABOUT THE AUTHOR

Although I, Robert Dominguez, the author and artist of *The Mysterious Final Flight Of MH-370*, while proud of my achievements, am ambivalent, in that, I take full responsibility for the failures for which I am solely to blame. Much like any American citizen.

As a youth, things were okay with two loving parents. Then, at the age of eight young years, my father expired to cancer. This sad event, probably, indirectly contributed to an early manhood. When I was ten years young, my surviving mother had a flat tire on her car. I managed to jack up her car, install the spare tire, and tighten all lug nuts for her and my safety as well as my older brother Augie and my younger sister Ann. This experience, I claim, led me to the realization that I had been born with an inherent talent for mechanical engineering and mechanizing those things, which needed repair or painting for my mother.

After earning my high school diploma, by good grades, I married my high school sweetheart, Debra Lee, who to this day is the most beautiful girl I had ever set my eyes on. Debra Lee was a girl who wore her heart on her sleeves, making her beauty visible both externally and internally. God blessed our union with three beautiful healthy children. Firstborn is my precious daughter, Jennifer Ann, our second child, my son Joseph Smith, and finally our next son, Jonathan Robert.

Being married with children led me to seek the highest-paying job, for which I was qualified, for good earning potential. This is when, at the age of twenty-two, I became an operating engineer of hugely enormous Earth-excavating and Earth-moving heavy equipment, in the land-developing endeavor, to both create new cities and/or enlarge preexisting cities with all contractors, civil engineers, land owners, land developers, and banks, working in harmony, under the watchful eye, and mine safety regulations, of both the US Army Corp of Engineers and MSHA (Mine Safety Hazard Administration). Yes, I became well compensated.

Then, after my ten-year loving relationship and marriage, one day, I awakened to an empty home, "an empty nest." After formal divorce proceedings, I was granted sole legal custody, as natural father of my three children. I immediately drove nonstop, from South Florida to Central California to reclaim my family. However, only my three children desired returning to our Florida home, bought and maintained, thanks to my operating engineer earnings.

As a sole father, I raised my three children, but during my working thirty years as an operating engineer, unfortunately, my two sons, Joseph and Jonathan, as teenagers, seventeen and sixteen, were involved in a horrific collision, involving the car they were passengers in and a speeding, fully-loaded tractor-trailer. Of course, the speeding 80 MPH tractor-trailer won the duel, resulting, according to the medical examiner, in instantaneous death to seventeen-year-old Joseph, and Jonathan becoming comatose. Jonathan awoke after four months of coma, emerging with a severe brain-stem injury and disability. For the next ten years in hospital, Jonathan steadily, but slowly, improved, allowing him to earn his high school diploma, and participate in his graduating class commencement ceremony! Joy! However, after Jonathan's ten-year fight, he succumbed to pathological cardiac arrest in his sleep, caused by the decade-earlier auto-truck collision, at the young age of twenty-six years. Sad unhappiness!

Later in life, I became a jet aircraft mechanic, for a fifteen-year span of time of jet aircraft repair experience. This is the era, when in 1993, the horrible collision occurred, taking both my two sons, Joseph and Jonathan in 2003, to heaven, at a ten-year interval, according to God's will. So I continued raising my surviving daughter, Jennifer Ann, meanwhile increasing my skills as a jet aircraft fuel systems/airframe repair specialist.

I actually moved to and fro, executing both trades, as the market conditions changed, to provide me and my family with the greatest earnings over a forty-five-year period of time, as a tax-paying citizen. Busy. Somehow, I found time to own and operate a landscaping company, while simultaneously becoming a US federal employee, all while raising my children. Busier!

My hobbies include writing, inventing time-saving beneficial products, with patents pending, and spending time with my daughter and two grandsons, either fishing or engaging in chess challenges, too many to count, and traveling our planet Earth's western hemisphere, sometimes co-mixed with career or solely with my family.

Lightning Source UK Ltd.
Milton Keynes UK
UKHW020211051221
394987UK00006B/235